Special Knits

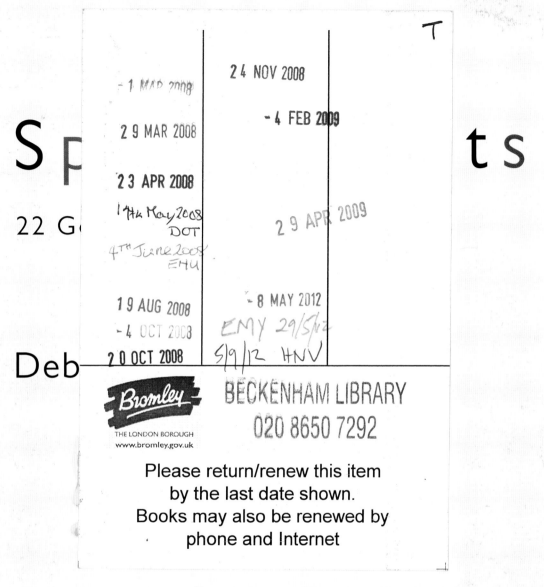

S p   t s

22 G

Deb

COLLINS & BROWN

First published in Great Britain in 2005
This paperback edition published in 2006 by
Collins & Brown
151 Freston Road
London
W10 6TH

An imprint of Anova Books Company Ltd

10 9 8 7 6 5 4 3 2 1

British Library Cataloguing-in-Publication Data:
A CIP catalogue record for this book is available from
the British Library

ISBN 1-84340-392-7

Edited and designed by Collins & Brown Limited

Editor: Kate Haxell
Designer: Roger Hammond
Photography: Sandra Lousada
Pattern checking: Rosy Tucker
Illustrations: Luise Roberts

Reproduction by Classicscan Pte Ltd
Printed in China

This book can be ordered direct from the publisher.
Contact the marketing department, but try your
bookshop first.

www.anovabooks.com

Contents

Introduction

Special Knits reflects our need to create beautiful handknits for babies in soft yarns that are gentle against delicate skin, each stitch invested with love and care by the knitter.

There are simple designs in this book where the special quality lies in the softness of the fabric, usually a cashmere mix. There are other projects where the uniqueness of the design comes from a scattering of beads, a velvet bow, or an organza ribbon that frames the gentle curve of a baby's cheek. In an age of the throwaway, these are garments that I hope will become the modern classic, knits to cherish and hand down through generations.

Most of the designs require little knowledge of complicated techniques; a simple garter-stitch blanket is perfect for a beginner and is given a touch of luxury with an edging of satin. Easy knits are embellished with decorative touches, while for those knitters who prefer more of a challenge, there is a sampler blanket or a cross-stitch embroidered gingham cardigan.

Debbie Bliss

eyelet vest

MEASUREMENTS

| To fit ages | 6–12 | 12–18 | 18–24 | 24–36 | months |

ACTUAL MEASUREMENTS

| Chest | 47 | 52 | 56 | 61 | cm |
| Length to shoulder | 28 | 31 | 34 | 40 | cm |

MATERIALS

- 2(3:3:4) 50g balls Debbie Bliss baby cashmerino in Mallard
- Pair each of 2¾mm and 3¼mm knitting needles
- 2¾mm circular knitting needle
- One button
- 1m narrow ribbon

TENSION

25 sts and 34 rows to 10cm square over st st using 3¼mm needles.

ABBREVIATIONS

See page 121.

BACK

With 2¾mm needles, cast on 81(89:97:105) sts.

K 3 rows.

Change to 3¼mm needles.

Beg with a k row work in st st until back measures 15(17:20:24)cm from cast on edge, ending with a p row.

Dec row K1, [k2tog, yf, skpo] 20(22:24:26) times. 61(67:73:79) sts.

Next row P to end.

Next row K2(0:3:1), * p2, k3; rep from * to last 4(2:5:3) sts, p2, k2(0:3:1).

These 2 rows form the rib patt.

Cont straight until back measures 18(20:23:27)cm from cast on edge, ending with a p row.

Shape armholes

Cast off 6 sts at beg of next 2 rows and 4 sts at beg of foll 2 rows. 41(47:53:59) sts.

Dec one st at each end of the next and every foll alt row until 31(37:43:49) sts rem.

P 1 row **.

Back opening

Next row Patt 14(17:20:23) sts, turn and work on these sts for first side of back opening, leave rem sts on a spare needle.

Next row Cast on 3 sts, k these 3 sts, then p to end.

Next row Patt to last 3 sts, k3.

Next row K3, p to end.

Rep the last 2 rows until back measures 25(28:31:37)cm from cast on edge, ending with a p row.

Shape neck

Next row Patt to last 6(8:8:10) sts, leave these sts on a holder, turn.

Dec one st at neck edge on every row until 5(7:9:11) sts rem.

Cont straight until back measures 28(31:34:40)cm from cast on edge, ending with a p row.

Shape shoulder

Cast off.

With right side facing, rejoin yarn to rem sts on spare needle, patt to end.

Next row P to last 3 sts, k3.

Next row K3, patt to end.

Rep the last 2 rows until back measures 25(28:31:37)cm from cast on edge, ending with a p row.

Shape neck

Next row Patt 6(8:8:10) sts, leave these sts on a holder, patt to end.

Dec one st at neck edge on every row until 5(7:9:11) sts rem.

Cont straight until back measures 28(31:34:40)cm from cast on edge, ending with a p row.

Shape shoulder

Cast off.

eyelet vest

FRONT

Work as given for Back to **.

Shape neck

Next row Patt 11(13:15:17) sts, turn and work on these sts for first side of neck shaping, leave rem sts on a spare needle.

Dec 1 st at neck edge on every foll alt row until 5(7:9:11) sts rem.

Cont without further shaping until front measures same as Back to shoulder, ending at side edge.

Shape shoulder

Cast off.

With right side facing, slip centre 9(11:13:15) sts onto a holder, rejoin yarn to rem sts on spare needle, patt to end.

Complete to match first side, reversing shaping.

NECKBAND

Join shoulder seams.

With right side facing and 2¾mm circular needle, slip 6(8:8:10) sts from left back holder onto needle, pick up and k9 sts up left back neck to shoulder, 17(17:18:19) sts down left front neck, k across 9(11:13:15) sts from front neck holder, pick up and k17(17:18:19) sts up right front neck to shoulder, 9 sts down right back neck, then k across 6(8:8:10) sts from right back holder. 73(79:83:91) sts.

Work backwards and forwards in rows.

K 1 row.

Buttonhole row (right side) K1, yf, k2tog, k to end.

K 1 row.

Cast off.

ARMBANDS

With right side facing and 2¾mm needles, pick up and k60(66:72:78) sts evenly around armhole edge.

K 3 rows.

Cast off.

TO FINISH

Join side and armband seams.

Lap button band behind buttonhole band and catch in place at centre back. Sew on button. Thread ribbon through eyelets to tie at centre front.

garter-stitch blanket

MEASUREMENTS

Approximately 55 x 74cm

MATERIALS

- Six 50g balls Debbie Bliss cashmerino aran in Pale Grey
- Pair of 5mm knitting needles
- Approximately 2.7 m of 5-cm wide satin ribbon

TENSION

18 sts and 36 rows to 10cm square over garter stitch using 5mm needles.

ABBREVIATIONS

See page 121.

TO MAKE

With 5mm needles, cast on 100 sts.
Work in garter stitch (k every row) until blanket measures 74cm from cast on edge.
Cast off.

EDGING

Press the ribbon in half along its length. Fold the ribbon over the edge of the blanket and working one side at a time, hand-stitch the edge of the ribbon to the blanket, folding in extra ribbon at the corners to form mitres. Fold under the end of the ribbon and slip stitch in place to neaten.

ribbed jacket

MEASUREMENTS

| To fit ages | | 0–3 | 3–6 | 6–9 | 9–12 | 12–24 | months |

ACTUAL MEASUREMENTS

Chest		46	51	55	60	64	cm
Length to shoulder		23	25	28	30	32	cm
Sleeve length		11	13	15	17	20	cm

MATERIALS

- 4(4:5:5:6) 50g balls of Debbie Bliss cashmerino aran in Pale Pink
- Pair of 5mm knitting needles
- Long circular 4½mm and 5mm knitting needles
- Optional decorative fastening

18 sts and 24 rows to 10cm square over st st using 5mm needles.

ABBREVIATIONS
See page 121.

BACK, FRONT AND SLEEVES
(worked in one piece)
With 5mm needles, cast on 44(48:52:56:60) sts.
Beg with a k row, work 32(34:38:40:44) rows in st st.
Change to 5mm circular needle.

Shape sleeves
Cast on 5(6:7:8:9) sts at beg of next 8 rows.
84(96:108:120:132) sts.
Work a further 16(18:22:24:26) rows.

Divide for fronts
Next row K34(40:45:51:56) sts, leave these sts on a spare needle, cast off next 16(16:18:18:20) sts, k to end.
Cont on last set of 34(40:45:51:56) sts only for left front.
Work a further 16(18:22:24:26) rows, so ending at sleeve edge.

Shape sleeve
Cast off 5(6:7:8:9) sts at beg of next and 3 foll alt rows. 14(16:17:19:20) sts.
Work 32(34:38:40:44) rows in st st.
Cast off.
With wrong side facing, rejoin yarn to rem sts on spare needle for right front, p to end.
Work a further 17(19:23:25:27) rows, so ending at sleeve edge.

Shape sleeve
Cast off 5(6:7:8:9) sts at beg of next and 3 foll alt rows. 14(16:17:19:20) sts.
Work 32(34:38:40:44) rows in st st.
Cast off.

EDGING
With right side facing and 4½mm circular needle, pick up and k46(50:54:58:62) sts evenly up right front, 22(22:26:26:30) sts from back neck and 46(50:54:58:62) sts evenly down left front. 114(122:134:142:154) sts.
1st row (wrong side) P2, * k2, p2; rep from * to end.
2nd row K2, * p2, k2; rep from * to end.
Rep the last 2 rows for 8(8:9:9:10)cm, ending with a 2nd row.
Cast off loosely but evenly in rib.

TO FINISH
Join side and sleeve seams.

r i b b e d   j a c k e t

hooded sweater

MEASUREMENTS

To fit ages	0–3	3–6	6–9	9–12	12–24	months

ACTUAL MEASUREMENTS

Chest	48	53	57	62	66	cm
Length to shoulder	24	26	28	30	34	cm
Sleeve length	14	16	18	20	22	cm

MATERIALS

• 4(4:5:5:6) 50g balls of Debbie Bliss cashmerino aran in Pale Blue

• Pair of 5mm knitting needles

18 sts and 24 rows to 10cm square over st st using 5mm needles.

ABBREVIATIONS

See page 121.

BACK

With 5mm needles, cast on 46(50:54:58:62) sts.
Beg with a k row work in st st until back measures 24(26:28:30:34)cm from cast on edge, ending with a p row.

Shape shoulders
Cast off 13(14:15:16:17) sts at beg of next 2 rows.
Cast off rem 20(22:24:26:28) sts.

FRONT

Work exactly as given for Back until 16 rows less than Back to shoulder have been worked.

Divide for front opening
Next row (right side) K23(25:27:29:31) sts, turn and work on these sts only for first side of front, leave rem sts on a spare needle.
Next row P to end.
Next row K21(23:25:27:29), m1, k2.
Next row P to end.
Next row K21(23:25:27:29), m1, k3.
Next row P to end.
Cont to inc one st as set on 5 foll right side rows.
30(32:34:36:38) sts.
P 1 row.
Shape shoulder
Next row (right side) Cast off 13(14:15:16:17) sts,
k a further 7(8:9:10:11) sts, m1, k to end.
Next row P18(19:20:21:22) sts, leave these sts on a holder.
With right side facing, rejoin yarn to rem sts on spare needle, k to end.
Next row P to end.
Next row K2, m1, k 21(23:25:27:29) sts.
Next row P to end.
Next row K3, m1, k 21(23:25:27:29) sts.
Cont to inc one st as set on 6 foll right side rows.
31(33:35:37:39) sts.
Next row (wrong side) Cast off 13(14:15:16:17) sts, p to end.

hooded sweater

cast on sts for back of hood
pick up and knit sts from back of hood

HOOD *make sure there is enough wool to finish hood.*

Next row (right side) [K10, m1, k8(9:10:11:12)] across sts of right front, cast on 38(40:42:44:46) sts for back, then [k8(9:10:11:12), m1, k10] across sts of left front. 76(80:84:88:92) sts.
Beg with a p row, work a further 35(37:39:41:43) rows in st st.
Cast off.

SLEEVES
With 5mm needles, cast on 30(32:34:36:38) sts.
Beg with a k row, work 8(8:10:10:12) rows in st st.
Inc row K3, m1, k to last 3 sts, m1, k3.
Beg with a p row, work 3 rows in st st.
Rep the last 4 rows until there are 42(46:50:54:58) sts.
Cont straight until sleeve measures 16(18:20:22:24)cm from cast on edge, ending with a p row.
Cast off.

TO FINISH
Join shoulder seams. With centre of cast off edge of sleeve to shoulder, sew on sleeves. Join side and sleeve seams. With right sides together fold hood in half and join cast off edges. Join cast on edge of hood to cast off sts of back neck.

embroidered kimono

MEASUREMENTS

To fit ages		3–6		6–12		12–18		months

ACTUAL MEASUREMENTS

Chest		54		58		61		cm
Length to shoulder		32		34		36		cm
Sleeve length		16		18		20		cm

MATERIALS

- 4(4:5) 50g balls of Debbie Bliss cotton cashmere in Teal (M)
- One 50g ball of Debbie Bliss cotton cashmere in Brown (C)
- Pair each of 3¼mm and 3¾mm knitting needles
- Oddments of pale blue and straw-coloured embroidery thread
- Embroidery needle

22 sts and 30 rows to 10cm square over st st using 3¾mm needles.

ABBREVIATIONS

See page 121.

BACK

With 3¼mm needles and C, cast on 72(76:80) sts.
K 3 rows.
Change to 3¾mm needles and M.
Beg with a k row work in st st.
Work 8(10:12) rows.
Dec row K8, skpo, k to last 10 sts, k2tog, k8.
Work 9 rows in st st.
Rep the last 10 rows 3 times more and the dec row again. 62(66:70) sts.
Cont straight until back measures 21(22:23)cm from cast on edge, ending with a p row.
Shape armholes
Cast off 5 sts at beg of next 2 rows. 52(56:60) sts.
Cont straight until back measures 32(34:36)cm from cast on edge, ending with a p row.
Shape shoulders
Cast off 7(7:8) sts at beg of next 2 rows and 6(7:7) sts at beg of foll 2 rows.
Leave rem 26(28:30) sts on a holder.

LEFT FRONT

With 3¼mm needles and C, cast on 58(60:62) sts.
K 3 rows.
Change to 3¾mm needles and M.
Beg with a k row work in st st.
Work 8(10:12) rows.
Dec row K8, skpo, k to end.
Work 9 rows in st st.
Rep the last 10 rows 3 times more and the dec row again. 53(55:57) sts.
Cont straight until front measures 21(22:23)cm from cast on edge, ending with a p row.
Shape armhole
Next row Cast off 5 sts, k to end. 48(50:52) sts.
P 1 row.
Shape neck
Next row K to last 8 sts, turn and leave these sts on a holder.
Next row Sl 1, p to end.
Next row K to last 6 sts, turn and leave these sts on the same holder.
Next row Sl 1, p to end.
Next row K to last 4 sts, turn and leave these sts on the same holder.
Next row Sl 1, p to end.
Next row K to last 2 sts, turn and leave these sts on the same holder.
Next row Sl 1, p to end.
Next row K to last 2 sts, k2tog.
Next row P2 tog, p to end.
Rep the last 2 rows until 13(14:15) sts rem.
Cont straight until front measures same as Back to shoulder, ending at armhole edge.

embroidered kimono

Shape shoulder

Cast off 7(7:8) sts at beg of next row.

Work 1 row.

Cast off rem 6(7:7) sts.

RIGHT FRONT

With 3¼mm needles and C, cast on 58(60:62) sts.

K 3 rows.

Change to 3¾mm needles and M.

Beg with a k row work in st st.

Work 8(10:12) rows.

Dec row K to last 10 sts, k2tog, k8.

Work 9 rows in st st.

Rep the last 10 rows 3 times more and the dec row again. 53(55:57) sts.

Cont straight until front measures 21(22:23)cm from cast on edge, ending with a k row.

Shape armhole

Next row Cast off 5 sts, p to end. 48(50:52) sts.

Next row K8 sts, leave these sts on a holder, k to end.

Next row P to last st, sl 1.

Next row K6 sts, leave these sts on the same holder, k to end.

Next row P to last st, sl 1.

Next row K4 sts, leave these sts on the same holder, k to end.

Next row P to last st, sl 1.

Next row K2 sts, leave these sts on the same holder, k to end.

Next row P to last st, sl 1.

Next row Skpo, k to end.

Next row P to last 2 sts, p2tog tbl.

Rep the last 2 rows until 13(14:15) sts rem.

Cont straight until front measures same as Back to shoulder, ending at armhole edge.

Shape shoulder

Cast off 7(7:8) sts at beg of next row.

Work 1 row.

Cast off rem 6(7:7) sts.

KEY

 STRAIGHT STITCH IN PALE BLUE OR STRAW

 STRAIGHT STITCH IN C

 CHAIN STITCH IN C

SLEEVES

With 3¼mm needles and C, cast on 34(36:38) sts.
K 3 rows.
Change to 3¾mm needles and M.
Beg with a k row, work in st st, inc one st at each end of the 3rd and every foll 6th row until there are 48(52:56) sts.
Cont straight until sleeve measures 16(18:20)cm from cast on edge, mark each end of last row with a coloured thread.
Work a further 2cm, ending with a p row.
Cast off.

RIGHT FRONT EDGING

With right side facing, 3¼mm needles and C, pick up and k44(46:48) sts evenly along right front straight edge.
K 3 rows.
Cast off.

LEFT FRONT EDGING

With right side facing, 3¼mm needles and C, pick up and k44(46:48) sts evenly along left front straight edge.
K 3 rows.
Cast off.

NECKBAND AND COLLAR

Join shoulder seams.
With right side facing, 3¼mm needles and C, pick up and k3 sts across row ends of right front band, k20 sts from right front holder, pick up and k27(29:31) sts up right front neck, k across 26(28:30) sts at back neck, pick up and k27(29:31) sts down left front neck, k20 sts from left front holder, pick up and k3 sts across row ends of left front band. 126(132:138) sts.
K 3 rows.
Next row Cast off 31(32:33) sts, k to last 31(32:33) sts, cast off these sts.
With wrong side facing, rejoin yarn to rem 64(68:72) sts, k to end.
Next row K2, skpo, k to last 4 sts, k2tog, k2.
Rep the last row 5 times more.
Cast off.

TO WORK EMBROIDERY

Using the diagram on page 25, work embroidered flower heads scattered randomly over all garment pieces. Work straight stitch petals with pale blue and straw embroidery thread and short straight stitch flower centres and lazy daisy sepals with C.

TO FINISH

Sew sleeves into armholes, with row ends above coloured threads sewn to cast off sts at underarm. Join side and sleeve seams. Sew 28cm of ribbon to end of right neckband. Sew 28cm of ribbon to left front level with right front tie. Make a crochet chain on end of left neckband and another on the inside of the right front at end of cast off sts of the armhole shaping to tie inside.

embroidered kimono

ribbon-edged cardigan

MEASUREMENTS

To fit ages	0–3	3–6	6–9	9–12	12–24	months

ACTUAL MEASUREMENTS

Chest	48	52	56	60	64	cm
Length to shoulder	21	24	26	28	32	cm
Sleeve length	13	15	17	19	22	cm

MATERIALS

- 2(3:3:4:4) 50g balls of Debbie Bliss baby cashmerino in Pale Pink
- Pair each of 3mm and 3¼mm knitting needles
- 6(6:6:6:7) buttons
- 60(70:70:80:80)cm ruffle-edged ribbon

TENSION

25 sts and 34 rows to 10cm square over st st using 3¼mm needles.

ABBREVIATIONS

See page 121.

BACK

With 3mm needles, cast on 62(67:72:77:82) sts.
K 5 rows.
Change to 3¼mm needles.
Next row (right side) K3, * p1, k4; rep from * to last 4 sts, p1, k3.
Next row P to end.
These 2 rows form the patt and are rep throughout.
Cont in patt until back measures 21(24:26:28:32)cm from cast on edge, ending with a p row.

Shape shoulders

Cast off 9(10:11:11:12) sts at beg of next 2 rows and 9(10:11:12:13) sts at beg of foll 2 rows.
Leave rem 26(27:28:31:32) sts on a spare needle.

LEFT FRONT

With 3mm needles, cast on 35(37:40:42:45) sts.
K 5 rows.
Change to 3¼mm needles.
Next row K3, * p1, k4; rep from * to last 7(9:7:9:7) sts, p1, k6(8:6:8:6).
Next row K5, p to end.
Rep the last 2 rows 22(27:32:32:39) times more.

Shape neck

Next row Patt to last 7(8:9:10:11) sts, leave these sts on a holder.

Dec one st at neck edge on every row until 18(20:22:23:25) sts rem.
Cont straight until front measures same as Back to shoulder, ending at armhole edge.

Shape shoulder

Cast off 9(10:11:11:12) sts at beg of next row.
Work 1 row.
Cast off rem 9(10:11:12:13) sts.

RIGHT FRONT

With 3mm needles, cast on 35(37:40:42:45) sts.
K 3 rows.
Next row (buttonhole row) (right side) K1, k2tog, yf, k to end.
K 1 row.
Change to 3¼mm needles.
Next row K6(8:6:8:6), * p1, k4; rep from * to last 4 sts, p1, k3.
Next row P to last 5 sts, k5.
Rep the last 2 rows 3(4:5:5:5) times more.
Next row (buttonhole row) K1, k2tog, yf, k3(5:3:5:3), * p1, k4; rep from * to last 4 sts, p1, k3.
Next row P to last 5 sts, k5.
Rep the last 10(12:14:14:14) rows 3(3:3:3:4) times more.
Next row K6(8:6:8:6), * p1, k4; rep from * to last 4 sts, p1, k3.
Next row P to last 5 sts, k5.
Rep the last 2 rows 2(3:4:4:4) times more.

Shape neck

Next row (right side) K7(8:9:10:11) sts, leave these sts on a holder, patt to end.
Dec one st at neck edge on every row until 18(20:22:23:25) sts rem.

ribbon-edged cardigan

Cont straight until front measures same as Back to shoulder, ending at armhole edge.

Shape shoulder

Cast off 9(10:11:11:12) sts at beg of next row.

Work 1 row.

Cast off rem 9(10:11:12:13) sts.

SLEEVES

With 3mm needles, cast on 29(33:35:39:39) sts.

K 5 rows.

Change to 3¼mm needles.

Next row K4(1:2:4:4), * p1, k4; rep from * to last 5(2:3:5:5) sts, p1, k4(1:2:4:4).

Next row P to end.

These 2 rows set the patt.

Cont in patt, **at the same time**, inc and work into patt

one st at each end of the next and every foll 4th row until there are 47(51:57:63:71) sts.

Cont straight until sleeve measures 13(15:17:19:22)cm from cast on edge, ending with a p row.

Cast off.

NECKBAND

Join shoulder seams.

With right side facing and 3mm needles, slip 7(8:9:10:11) sts from right front neck holder onto a needle, pick up and k16(16:17:17:18) sts up right front neck, k26(27:28:31:32) sts from back neck holder, pick up and k16(16:17:17:18) sts down left front neck, k7(8:9:10:11) from left front holder. 72(75:80:85:90) sts.

K 1 row.

Next row (buttonhole row) K1, k2tog, yf, k to end.

K 3 rows.

Cast off.

TO FINISH

Matching centre of cast off edge of sleeve to shoulder, sew on sleeves. Join side and sleeve seams. Sew on buttons. Sew ribbon behind buttonhole band and around neck edge.

rabbit

MEASUREMENTS
Approximately 28cm, excluding ears

MATERIALS
- Two 50g balls of Debbie Bliss cashmerino aran in Duck Egg
- Small amount of cream yarn for pom-pom tail
- Pair of 3¼mm knitting needles
- Washable polyester toy stuffing
- Grey embroidery wool for features

TENSION
23 sts and 32 rows to 10cm square over st st using 3¼mm needles.

ABBREVIATIONS
m1L = inserting left needle from the front, lift strand between sts and k into back of it so base of made st slants to the left.
m1R = inserting left needle from the back, lift strand between sts and k into front of it so base of made st slants to the right.
Also see page 121.

FACE

With 3¼mm needles, cast on 9 sts.

1st row (right side) Kfb, k6, kfb, k1.

2nd row and every wrong side row P.

3rd row Kfb, k4, m1R, k1, m1L, k3, kfb, k1. 15 sts.

5th row Kfb, k6, m1R, k1, m1L, k5, kfb, k1. 19 sts.

7th row Kfb, k8, m1R, k1, m1L, k7, kfb, k1. 23 sts.

9th row Kfb, k9, m1R, k3, m1L, k8, kfb, k1. 27 sts.

11th row Kfb, k10, m1R, k5, m1L, k9, kfb, k1. 31 sts.

13th row K11, k2tog, k5, skpo, k11. 29 sts.

15th row K10, k2tog, k5, skpo, k10. 27 sts.

17th row K1, k2tog, k6, k2tog, k5, skpo, k6, skpo, k1. 23 sts.

19th row K1, k2tog, k4, k2tog, k5, skpo, k4, skpo, k1. 19 sts.

21st row K1, k2tog, k2, k2tog, k5, skpo, k2, skpo, k1. 15 sts.

23rd row K1, [k2tog] twice, k5, [skpo] twice, k1. 11 sts.

P 1 row.

Cast off.

BACK

Gusset

With 3¼mm needles, cast on 22 sts.

Beg with a k row, work 6 rows in st st.

Cont in st st, dec one st at each end of next 8 rows. 6 sts.

Cast off.

Back

With right side facing, pick up and k42 sts around shaped edge of gusset.

Beg with a p row, work 15 rows in st st.

Dec row (right side) K1, [k2tog] 10 times, [skpo] 10 times, k1. 22 sts.

Beg with a p row, work 11 rows in st st.

Shape armholes

Cast off 2 sts at beg of next 2 rows. 18 sts.

Dec row (right side) K1, k2tog, k to last 3 sts, skpo, k1. 16 sts.

Work 5 rows in st st.

Shape shoulders

Cast off 3 sts at beg of next 2 rows. 10 sts.

Work 2 rows in st st.

Shape back of head

Inc row (right side) Kfb, k to last 2 sts, kfb, k1. 12 sts.

Cont in st st, inc in this way at each end of next 3 right side rows. 18 sts.

Work 5 rows in st st.

Dec one st at each end of next row and 4 foll right side rows. 8 sts.

Cast off.

FRONT

With 3¼mm needles, cast on 22 sts.

Beg with a k row, work 16 rows in st st.

Dec one st at each end of next row. 20 sts.

Work 11 rows in st st.

Shape armholes

Cast off 2 sts at beg of next 2 rows. 16 sts.

Dec row (right side) K1, k2tog, k to last 3 sts, skpo, k1. 14 sts.

Work 5 rows in st st.

Shape shoulders

Cast off 2 sts at beg of next 2 rows. 10 sts.

 rabbit

Dec row (right side) K1, k2tog, k to last 3 sts, skpo, k1. 8 sts.
Work 2 rows in st st.
Cast off.

LEGS

(make 2)
With 3¼mm needles, cast on 5 sts.
1st row (right side) [Kfb] 4 times, k1. 9 sts.
P 1 row.
Inc one st at each end of next row and foll 2 right side rows. 15 sts.
Work 17 rows in st st **.
Shape thighs
1st row (right side) K6, [kfb] twice, k7. 17 sts.
Working one more st before and after incs, inc 2 sts in this way at centre of next 5 right side rows. 27 sts.
Work 9 rows in st st.
Next row (right side) K11, skpo, k1, k2tog, k11. 25 sts.
P 1 row.
Next row (right side) K10, skpo, k1, k2tog, k10. 23 sts.
P 1 row.
Cast off.

ARMS

(make 2)
Work as given for Legs to **.
Shape top
Cast off 2 sts at beg of next 2 rows. 11 sts.
Dec one st at each end of next row. 9 sts.
P 1 row.
Cast off.

EARS

(make 2)
With 3¼mm needles, cast on 7 sts.
1st row (right side) Kfb, k to last 2 sts, kfb, k1. 9 sts.
2nd row K1, p to last st, k1.
Cont in st st with k1 edge sts, inc one st at each end of next 3 right side rows. 15 sts.
Work 31 rows straight.
Dec row (right side) K2, skpo, k to last 4 sts, k2tog, k2. 13 sts.
Dec in this way at each end of next 2 right side rows. 9 sts.
Work 1 row.
Cast off.

TO FINISH

Join inside leg seams. Stuff legs. Flatten tops of legs and slip stitch closed. Join back to front at side seams. Sew legs to cast on edge of front, then to cast on edge of back. Join arm seams. Stuff arms. Stuff body to armholes. Join shoulders and set in arms. Add more stuffing to body through neck hole. Fold cast on edge of face in half and join for chin seam. Join face to back of head, leaving a gap at the top. Stuff face. Roll cast off edges of ears and set ears into gap at top of head, closing seam between ears. Add more stuffing to head. Join face to neck.

Using grey embroidery thread and face shaping as a guide to placing features, embroider nose, mouth and eyes, pulling thread through head to indent eyes slightly.

Make a pom-pom from cream yarn and sew on for tail.

alphabet sweater

MEASUREMENTS

To fit ages	3	6	12	24	months

ACTUAL MEASUREMENTS

Chest	54	59	64	69	cm
Length to shoulder	26.5	29.5	33	37.5	cm
Sleeve length	16	19	22	25	cm

MATERIALS

- 4(5:5:6) 50g balls of Debbie Bliss cashmerino aran in Teal
- Pair each of 3¼mm, 3¾mm and 4½mm knitting needles
- Cable needle
- 3 buttons
- Contrast embroidery yarn

24 sts and 26 rows to 10cm square over twist patt
using 4½mm needles.

ABBREVIATIONS

C3B = slip next st on to cable needle, hold at back,
k2, then k1 from cable needle.

C3F = slip next 2 sts on to cable needle, hold at front,
k1, then k2 from cable needle.

C3Bp = slip next st on to cable needle, hold at back,
k2, then p1 from cable needle.

C3Fp = slip next 2 sts on to cable needle, hold at
front, p1, then k2 from cable needle.

C3Bpp = slip next 2 sts on to cable needle, hold at
back, p1, then p2 from cable needle.

C3Fpp = slip next st on to cable needle, hold at front,
p2, then p1 from cable needle.

C3Bkp = slip next 2 sts on to cable needle, hold at
back, k1, then p2 from cable needle.

C3Fpk = slip next st on to cable needle, hold at front,
p2, then k1 from cable needle.

C4B = slip next 2 sts on to cable needle, hold at back,
k2, then k2 from cable needle.

T2R = k into front of 2nd st, then into front of 1st st,
slip 2 sts off left needle tog.

T2L = insert right needle tip from the back between
sts to k into front of 2nd st, then k into front of 1st st,
slip 2 sts off left needle tog.

Also see page 121.

BACK

With 3¼mm needles, cast on 66(72:78:84) sts.

K 6 rows.

Change to 3¾mm needles.

1st row (right side) P1, [k2, p1] 10(11:12:13) times,
k4, [p1, k2] 10(11:12:13) times, p1.

2nd, 4th and 6th rows K1, [p2, k1] 10(11:12:13)
times, p4, [k1, p2] 10(11:12:13) times, k1.

3rd row P1, [k2, p1] 10(11:12:13) times, C4B,
[p1, k2] 10(11:12:13) times, p1.

5th row As 1st row.

Change to 4½mm needles.

1st row (right side) P1, [T2R, p1] 10(11:12:13) times,
C4B, [p1, T2L] 10(11:12:13) times, p1.

2nd row K1, [p2, k1] 10(11:12:13) times, p4, [k1, p2]
10(11:12:13) times, k1.

3rd row (right side) P1, [T2R, p1] 10(11:12:13)
times, k4, [p1, T2L] 10(11:12:13) times, p1.

4th row As 2nd row.

These 4 rows form centre cable with twist patt at
each side **.

Patt 32(38:42:48) more rows.

Shape armholes

Cast off 6 sts at beg of next 2 rows. 54(60:66:72) sts.

Patt 24(26:30:36) more rows.

Cast off.

alphabet sweater

FRONT

Work as given for Back to **.

Patt 18(26:30:42) more rows.

Work diamond as folls:

1st row (right side) Patt 30(33:36:39), C3B, C3F, patt 30(33:36:39).

2nd row Patt 29(32:35:38), C3Fpp, p2, C3Bpp, patt 29(32:35:38).

3rd row Patt 28(31:34:37), C3B, k4, C3F, patt 28(31:34:37).

4th row Patt 27(30:33:36), C3Fpp, p6, C3Bpp, patt 27(30:33:36).

5th row Patt 26(29:32:35), C3B, k8, C3F, patt 26(29:32:35).

6th row Patt 25(28:31:34), C3Fpp, p10, C3Bpp, patt 25(28:31:34).

All sizes, but shape armholes on 4th size only

7th row Patt 24(27:30:cast off 6 sts, patt next 26 sts), C3B, k12, C3F, patt 24(27:30:33).

8th row Patt 23(26:29:cast off 6 sts, patt next 25 sts), C3Fpp, p14, C3Bpp, patt 23(26:29:26). 66(72:78:72) sts.

9th row Patt 22(25:28:25), C3B, k16, C3F, patt 22(25:28:25).

10th row Patt 21(24:27:24), C3Fpp, p18, C3Bpp, patt 21(24:27:24).

11th row Patt 20(23:26:23), C3B, k20, C3F, patt 20(23:26:23).

12th row Patt 19(22:25:22), C3Fpp, p22, C3Bpp, patt 19(22:25:22).

All sizes, but shape armholes on 2nd and 3rd sizes only

13th row (right side) Patt 19(cast off 6 sts, patt next 15 sts:cast off 6 sts, patt next 18 sts:patt 22), k28, patt 19(16:19:22).

14th row Patt 19(cast off 6 sts, patt next 15 sts:cast off 6 sts, patt next 18 sts:patt 22), C3Bpp, p22, C3Fpp, patt 19(16:19:22). 66(60:66:72) sts.

All sizes, but shape armholes on 1st size only

15th row (right side) Cast off 6 sts, patt next 13 sts(patt 17:patt 20:patt 23), C3F, k20, C3B, patt 20(17:20:23).

16th row Cast off 6 sts, patt next 14 sts(patt 18: patt 21:patt 24), C3Bkp, p18, C3Fpk, patt 15(18:21:24). 54(60:66:72) sts.

17th row Patt 16(19:22:25), C3F, k16, C3B, patt 16(19:22:25).

18th row Patt 17(20:23:26), C3Bpp, p14, C3Fpp, patt 17(20:23:26).

19th row Patt 18(21:24:27), C3Fp, k12, C3Bp, patt 18(21:24:27).

20th row Patt 19(22:25:28), C3Bpp, p10, C3Fpp, patt 19(22:25:28).

21st row Patt 20(23:26:29), C3F, k8, C3B, patt 20(23:26:29).

22nd row Patt 21(24:27:30), C3Bkp, p6, C3Fpk, patt 21(24:27:30).

23rd row Patt 22(25:28:31), C3F, k4, C3B, patt 22(25:28:31).

24th row Patt 23(26:29:32), C3Bpp, p2, C3Fpp, patt 23(26:29:32).

25th row Patt 24(27:30:33), C3Fp, C3Bp, patt 24(27:30:33).

26th row Patt 25(28:31:34), p4, patt 25(28:31:34).

27th row Patt 25(28:31:34), C4B, patt 25(28:31:34).

Work 5 more rows in twist patt with centre cable.

Shape neck

Next row (wrong side) Patt 19(19:22:25) turn and cont on these sts only, leave rem sts on spare needle.
Dec one st at neck edge on next 6 rows.
13(13:16:19) sts.
Patt 1(1:5:5) rows.
Cast off.
With right side facing, slip centre 16(22:22:22) sts onto a holder, rejoin yarn to rem sts, patt to end.
19(19:22:25) sts.
Complete to match first side.

SLEEVES

With 3¼mm needles, cast on 36(36:42:42) sts.
K 6 rows.
Change to 3¾mm needles.
1st row (right side) P1, [k2, p1] 5(5:6:6) times, k4, [p1, k2] 5(5:6:6) times, p1.
This row sets patt to match Back.
Cont in patt, work 5 more rows.
Change to 4½mm needles.
1st row (right side) P1, [T2R, p1] 5(5:6:6) times, C4B, [p1, T2L] 5(5:6:6) times, p1.
This row sets patt to match Back.
Cont in patt, work 5 more rows.
Inc and take into patt one st at each end of next row, then on 5(8:8:11) foll 4th rows. 48(54:60:66) sts.
Patt 11(7:15:11) rows.
Cast off.

NECKBAND

Join right shoulder seam and mark position of left shoulder on back edge. With right side facing and 3¼mm needles, pick up and k10(10:13:13) sts down left front neck, patt 6(9:9:9), [k2tog] twice, patt 6(9:9:9) from front neck holder, pick up and k10(10:13:13) sts up right front neck and 27(33:33:33) sts across back neck to marker. 61(73:79:79) sts.
K 3 rows.
Next row (right side) P1, [k2, p1] to end.
Rib 6 more rows.
Next row (wrong side) P.
Work 4 more rows in st st.
Cast off knitwise.

SHOULDER EDGING

With right side facing and 3¼mm needles, pick up and k17(17:25:25) sts across left front shoulder and neckband.
Cast off knitwise.
Make 3 button loops on edging.

TO FINISH

Join end of left shoulder. Set in sleeves, sewing row ends at top of sleeve to cast off sts at underarms. Join side and sleeve seams. Using alphabet chart from Sampler Blanket on page 86 and contrast yarn, embroider your chosen letter in the front diamond using cross stitch, adapting curlicues to fit. Sew buttons onto back left shoulder.

alphabet sweater

check and cross-stitch jacket

MEASUREMENTS

To fit ages	6	18	24	months

ACTUAL MEASUREMENTS

Chest	55	62	69	cm
Length	26	33	42	cm
Sleeve	17	24	31	cm

MATERIALS

• 2(3:4) 50g balls of Debbie Bliss cotton cashmere in Cream (D) and one 50g ball in each of Magenta (A), Pink (B), Lilac (C), Purple (E), Grey-blue (F) and Navy (G)

• Pair each of 3¼mm and 4mm knitting needles

• One button

• 1m narrow ribbon

23 sts and 28 rows to 10cm square over eyelet, band and gingham patt using 4mm needles.

ABBREVIATIONS
pfb = p into front and back of st.
wyab = with yarn at back of work.
wyif = with yarn in front of work.
Also see page 121.

NOTE
When counting rows, remember that each gingham band takes 16 rows to work, but it looks less because of the slipped stitches.

BACK AND FRONTS
With 3¼mm needles and A, cast on
135(151:167) sts.
1st row (right side) P1, [k1, p1] to end.
Change to B.
2nd row K1, [p1, k1] to end.
These 2 rows form rib.
Rib 1 more row B, 2 rows C and 3 rows D **.
Next row Rib to end and dec one st in centre of row.
134(150:166) sts.
Next row (wrong side) Rib 4, kfb and leave these
6 sts on a holder for button band, k to last 5 sts, turn and leave these 5 sts on a holder for buttonhole band.
124(140:156) sts.
Change to 4mm needles.
1st row (right side) K.
2nd row P2, [yo, p2tog] to end.
3rd row K.

4th row (wrong side) With 3¼mm needles,
k to end.
Change to 4mm needles.
5th row K.
6th row P.
7th row K.
8th row P.
9th row With 3¼mm needles, p to end.
Change to 4mm needles.
10th row P.
11th row With C, k3, [sl2 wyb, k2] to last st, k1.
12th row With E, sl3 wyif, [p2, sl2 wyif] to last st, sl1 wyif.
13th row With E, sl3 wyab, [k2, sl2 wyab] to last st, sl1.
14th row With C, p.
15th row With D, k3, [sl2 wyab, k2] to last st, k1.
16th row With D, p3, [sl2 wyif, p2] to last st, p1.
17th row With C, k.
18th row As 12th row.
19th row As 13th row.
20th row As 14th row.
21st row As 15th row.
22nd row As 16th row.
23rd row As 17th row.
24th row As 12th row.
25th row As 13th row.
26th row With C, p3, [sl2 wyif, p2] to last st, p1.
Cont in D.
27th row K.
28th row With 3¼mm needles, k to end.
These 28 rows form the patt.
Using F for C and G for E on alternate bands of

check and cross-stitch jacket

check patt, work these 28 rows 0(1:2) times more, then work 1st to 9th rows again.

Divide for back and fronts

Next row (wrong side) With D, p27(31:35) for left front, cast off 6 sts, p until there are 58(66:74) sts on right needle after cast off sts, cast off 6 sts, p to end for right front.

Right front

Shape armhole

Cont in check patt and dec one st at beg of 4th row, then at armhole edge on 3 foll 3rd rows. 23(27:31) sts.

Patt 3 rows.

Leave sts on a holder.

Back

Shape armholes

With right side facing, rejoin yarn to centre 58(66:74) sts, cont in check patt and dec one st at each end of 4th row and 3 foll 3rd rows. 50(58:66) sts.

Patt 3 rows.

Leave sts on a holder.

Left front

Shape armhole

With right side facing, rejoin yarn to rem 27(31:35) sts, cont in check patt and dec one st at end of 4th row, then at armhole edge on 3 foll 3rd rows. 23(27:31) sts.

Patt 3 rows.

Leave sts on a holder.

SLEEVES

With 3¼mm needles and A, cast on 41(45:49) sts.

Work as given for Back and Fronts to **.

Rib 1 more row D.

Cont in D.

Next row (wrong side) K.

Change to 4mm needles.

1st row (right side) K.

2nd row P1, [yo, p2tog] to end.

3rd row K.

4th row With 3¼mm needles, k to end.
Change to 4mm needles.

5th row K.

6th row P.

7th row K to last 2 sts, kfb, k1. 42(46:50) sts.

8th row P.

9th row With 3¼mm needles, p to end.
Change to 4mm needles.

10th row P.

11th row With C, k2, [sl2 wyb, k2] to end.

12th row With E, sl2 wyif, [p2, sl2 wyif] to end.

13th row With E, sl2 wyab, [k2, sl2 wyab] to end.

14th row With C, p.

15th row With D, k2, [sl2 wyab, k2] to end.

16th row With D, p2, [sl2 wyif, p2] to end.

17th row With C, kfb, k to last 2 sts, kfb, k1.
44(48:52) sts.

18th row With E, sl3 wyif, [p2, sl2 wyif] to last st,
sl1 wyif.

19th row With E, sl3 wyab, [k2, sl2 wyab] to last st,
sl1 wyab.

20th row With C, p.

21st row With D, k3, [sl2 wyab, k2] to last st, k1.

22nd row With D, p3, [sl2 wyif, p2] to last st, p1.

23rd row With C, kfb, k to last 2 sts, kfb, k1.
46(50:54) sts.

24th row With E, p2, [sl2 wyif, p2] to end.

25th row With E, k2, [sl2 wyab, k2] to end.

26th row With C, sl2 wyif, [p2, sl2 wyif] to end.
Cont in D.

27th and 28th rows K.

Using F for C and G for E on alternate bands of
check patt and ending the 2nd patt row p1, work

these 28 rows 0(1:2) times more, omitting incs, then
work 1st to 8th rows.

Shape top

Cont in patt in D and cast off 4 sts at beg of next
2 rows.

Cont in check patt, beg k2 F(C:F), dec one st at each
end of 4th row and 3 foll 3rd rows. 30(34:38) sts.

Patt 3 rows.

Leave sts on a holder.

YOKE

Joining row With right side facing, 4mm needles and
D, work [k21(25:29), skpo] across right front sts,
[k2tog, k26(30:34), skpo] across right sleeve sts,
[k2tog, k46(54:62), skpo] across back sts, [k2tog,
k26(30:34), skpo] across left sleeve sts, then work
[k2tog, k21(25:29)]across left front sts.
148(172:196) sts.

K 1 row.

1st dec row (right side) K2(1:2), [k2tog, k14(13:12),
skpo] 8(10:12) times, k2(1:2). 132(152:172) sts.

Patt 3 rows.

2nd dec row (right side) K1, [k2tog, k6, skpo]
13(15:17) times, k1. 106(122:138) sts.

K 1 row.

3rd dec row (right side) K1, [k2tog, k4, skpo]
13(15:17) times, k1.
80(92:104) sts.

Patt 21 rows, so ending k 1 row D.

Cont in D.

4th dec row (right side) K1, [k2tog, k2, skpo]
13(15:17) times, k1.
54(62:70) sts.

check and cross-stitch jacket

Patt 3(3:9) rows.
Leave sts on a holder.

BUTTON BAND

With right side facing, 3¼mm needles and D, rib 6 sts
from left front holder.
Cont in rib until band, when slightly stretched fits up
front edge to neck.
Leave sts on a holder.
Sew on band.
Place a marker for button 5cm down from neck edge.

BUTTONHOLE BAND

With wrong side facing, 3¼mm needles and D, cast
on one st, rib 5 sts from right front holder. 6 sts.
Cont to match button band, making buttonhole
opposite marker as folls:
Buttonhole row (right side) P1, k1, yo, k2tog, p1, k1.

NECKBAND

With right side facing, 3¼mm needles and D, beg at
right front, [p1, k1] twice, p2tog from buttonhole
band holder, work [k1, p1] to last 2 sts, skpo, from
yoke holder, then work p2tog, [k1, p1] twice from
buttonband holder. 63(71:79) sts.
1st row (wrong side) P2, [k1, p1] to last st, p1.
Rib 1 more row D, 2 rows B and 1 row A.
With A, cast off in rib.

RIGHT FRONT EDGING

With 3¼mm needles and B, beg and end with B rows
at lower edge and neck, pick up and k55(71:93) sts up
right front edge.

Beg k1, rib 1 row.
Change to A and rib 1 row.
Cast off purlwise.

LEFT FRONT EDGING

Work as Right Front Edging, on left front edge.

WORK EMBROIDERY

Work large cross stitches on alternate stocking stitch
bands using A and pairs of chain stitches using B.

TO FINISH

Join underarm and sleeve seams. Join ends of front
edgings. Slot ribbon through eyelet holes on yoke and
secure ends. Sew on button.

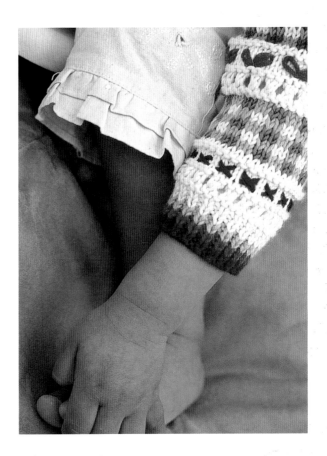

ribbon-tied dress

MEASUREMENTS

To fit ages	3–6	6–12	12–18	18–24	months

ACTUAL MEASUREMENTS

Chest	50	56	62	67	cm
Length to shoulder	37	44	48	52	cm
Sleeve length	15	18	20	22	cm

MATERIALS

- 4(5:5:6) 50g balls Debbie Bliss baby cashmerino in White
- Pair each of 3mm and 3¼mm knitting needles
- 1.5m ribbon

TENSION

25 sts and 34 rows to 10cm square over st st using 3¼mm needles.

ABBREVIATIONS

See page 121.

BACK

With 3mm needles, cast on 96(103:112:121) sts.
K 3 rows.
Change to 3¼mm needles.
Beg with a k row work 6 rows in st st.
Dec row K12(13:14:15), skpo, k to last 14(15:16:17) sts, k2tog, k12(13:14:15).
Work 7(9:9:9) rows in st st.
Rep the last 8(10:10:10) rows 9(9:10:11) times more. 76(83:90:97) sts.
Cont straight until back measures 25(31:34:37)cm from cast on edge, ending with a right side row.
Dec row P5, [p2tog, p5] 9(10:11:12) times, p2tog, p6. 66(72:78:84) sts. **
Cont straight until back measures 28(34:37:40)cm from cast on edge, ending with a p row.

Shape armholes

Cast off 8(9:10:11) sts at beg of next 2 rows. 50(54:58:62) sts.
Cont straight until back measures 37(44:48:52)cm from cast on edge, ending with a p row.

Shape shoulders

Cast off 10(11:12:13) sts at beg of next 2 rows.
Cast off rem 30(32:34:36) sts.

FRONT

Work as given for Back to **.

Divide for front opening

Next row (right side) K24(26:28:30), turn and work on these sts for first side of neck, leave rem sts on a spare needle.
Next row Cast on 18(20:22:24) sts, k3, p2tog, p to end. 41(45:49:53) sts.
Next row K to last 4 sts, k2tog, k2.
Next row K3, p2tog, p to end.
Rep the last 2 rows 3 times more.

Shape armhole

Next row Cast off 8(9:10:11) sts, k to last 4 sts, k2tog, k2.
Next row K3, p to end.
Next row K to last 4 sts, k2tog, k2.
Cont to dec at neck edge on every alt row until 13(14:15:16) sts rem.
Cont without further shaping until front measures same as Back to shoulder, ending at armhole edge.

Shape shoulder

Cast off 10(11:12:13) sts at beg of next row.
Cont in garter st on rem 3 sts until band fits halfway across back neck.
Cast off.
With right side facing, rejoin yarn to rem sts, k18(20:22:24) sts, turn and work on these sts only.
Next row K1, p to last 5 sts, p2tog tbl, k3.
Next row K2, skpo, k to end.
Leave these sts on a spare needle.
Rejoin yarn to rem 24(26:28:30) sts, k to end.
Next row P to last st, k1.
Next row K to end.

ribbon-tied dress

Next row P to end, then work across sts on spare needle as folls: p to last 5 sts, p2tog tbl, k3. Complete to match first side.

SLEEVES

With 3mm needles, cast on 36(38:42:46) sts.
K 5 rows.
Change to 3¼mm needles.
Beg with a k row work in st st and inc one st at each end of the 3rd and every foll 6th row until there are 50(56:60:66) sts.
Cont straight until sleeve measures 15(18:20:22)cm from cast on edge, ending with a p row.
Mark each end of last row then work a further 6(6:8:8) rows.
Cast off.

TO FINISH

Join cast off edges of 3-st band, sew to back neck edge. With centre of cast off edge of sleeve to shoulder, sew sleeves into armholes with row ends above markers sewn to cast off sts at underarm. Sew cast on sts of left front behind right front. Join side and sleeve seams. Cut ribbon in half. Sew one end of each length to front edges. Thread left front ribbon through eyelet, take both ribbons around the back and bring forward to tie at centre front.

shawl

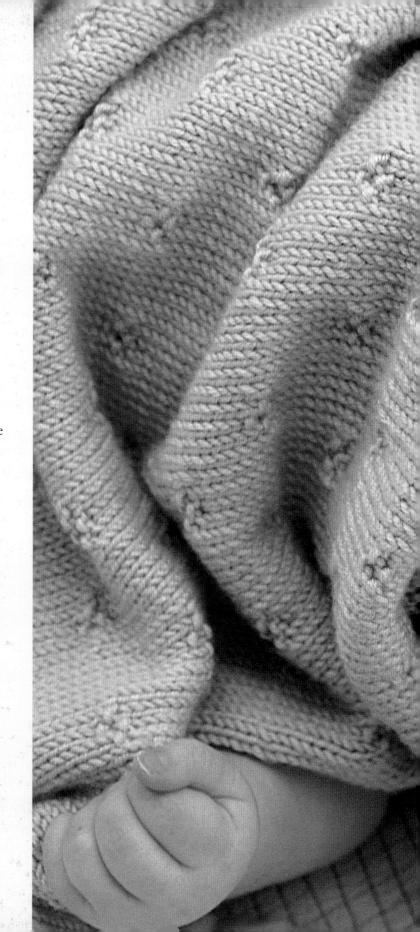

MEASUREMENTS

Approximately 69 x 72cm

MATERIALS

• Six 50g balls of Debbie Bliss baby cashmerino in Pale Blue
• Pair of 3¼mm knitting needles

25 sts and 34 rows to 10cm square over st st using 3¼mm needles.

ABBREVIATIONS
See page 121.

CENTRAL SQUARE
With 3¼mm needles, cast on 159 sts.
Moss st row K1, [p1, k1] to end.
Rep this row 3 times more.
5th row (right side) [K1, p1] 4 times, * k3, [p1, k1] 3 times, p1; rep from * to last 11 sts, k3, [p1, k1] 4 times.
6th row (wrong side) [K1, p1] 3 times, k1, * p5, [k1, p1] twice, k1; rep from * to last 12 sts, p5, [k1, p1] 3 times, k1.
7th row [K1, p1] 3 times, * k7, p1, k1, p1; rep from * to last 3 sts, k1, p1, k1.
8th row [K1, p1] twice, k1, * p9, k1; rep from * to last 4 sts, [p1, k1] twice.
9th row [K1, p1] twice, k to last 4 sts, [p1, k1] twice.
10th row K1, p1, k1, p to last 3 sts, k1, p1, k1.
11th row As 9th row.
12th row [K1, p1] twice, k1, p to last 5 sts, [k1, p1] twice, k1.
13th row [K1, p1] 3 times, k to last 6 sts, [p1, k1] 3 times.
14th row [K1, p1] 3 times, k1, * p7, k1, p2; rep from * to last 12 sts, p5, [k1, p1] 3 times, k1.
15th row [K1, p1] 4 times, * k5, p1, k1, p1, k2; rep from * to last 11 sts, k3, [p1, k1] 4 times.
16th row As 14th row.

17th row As 13th row.
18th row As 12th row.
19th row As 9th row.
20th row As 10th row.
21st row As 9th row.
22nd row As 12th row.
23rd row As 13th row.
24th row [K1, p1] 3 times, k1, p12, * k1, p9; rep from * to last 10 sts, p3, [k1, p1] 3 times, k1.
25th row [K1, p1] 4 times, k10, * p1, k1, p1, k7; rep from * to last 11 sts, k3, [p1, k1] 4 times.
26th row As 24th row.
27th row As 13th row.
28th row As 12th row.
The last 20 rows (9th to 28th patt rows) form the patt and are repeated 9 times more.
Now work a further 11 rows, so ending with a 19th patt row.
Next 8 rows Work 8th, 7th, 6th, 5th, 4th, 3rd, 2nd, and 1st rows.
Cast off knitwise.

s h a w l

EDGING

With 3¼mm needles, cast on 6 sts.

1st row K2, yf, k2tog, yf, k to end.

2nd row K all sts.

3rd to 13th rows Rep 1st and 2nd rows 5 times more, then the 1st row again. 13 sts.

14th row Cast off 7 sts, k to end. 6 sts.

These 14 rows form the edging patt and are repeated until straight edge fits all around the shawl edge, ending with a 13th row. Slip stitch edging in place to edge of shawl in short sections as you knit, easing to fit around the corners. Cast off all sts.

picot dress and bag

MEASUREMENTS

To fit ages	3–6	9–12	12–18	18–24	months

ACTUAL MEASUREMENTS

Chest	47	52	56	61	cm
Length to shoulder	36	41	49	55	cm

MATERIALS

• Dress: 4(5:6:7) 50g balls Debbie Bliss baby cashmerino in Lilac
• Bag: One 50g ball Debbie Bliss baby cashmerino in Lilac
• Pair each of 2¾mm and 3¼mm knitting needles
• 2¾mm circular knitting needle
• 1 button
• 30cm of narrow ribbon for dress and 1.5m narrow ribbon for bag

TENSION

25 sts and 34 rows to 10cm square over st st using 3¼mm needles.

ABBREVIATIONS

ssk = [slip 1 knitwise] twice, insert tip of left needle into fronts of slipped sts and k2tog.
kp = knit and purl into next st.
pk = purl and knit into next st.
Also see page 121.

DRESS BACK

** With 3¼mm needles, cast on
101(109:117:125) sts.

Moss st row K1, [p1, k1] to end.

Rep this row 5 times more.

Beg with a k row work 6 rows in st st.

Dec row (right side) K10(11:12:13), ssk, k to last
12(13:14:15) sts, k2tog, k10(11:12:13).

Work 5(7:9:11) rows in st st.

Rep the last 6(8:10:12) rows until 81(89:97:105) sts rem.

Cont straight until back measures 23(27:34:39)cm
from cast on edge, ending with a p row.

Dec row K1, [k2tog, k2] 20(22:24:26) times.
61(67:73:79) sts.

Moss st row K1, [p1, k1] to end.

Cont straight in moss st until back measures
26(30:37:42)cm from cast on edge, ending with a
wrong side row.

Shape armholes

Cast off 6 sts at beg of next 2 rows and 4 sts at beg of
foll 2 rows.

Dec one st at each end of the next and every foll alt
row until 31(37:43:49) sts rem.

Moss st 1 row. **

Back opening

Next row Moss st 14(17:20:23) sts, turn and work on
these sts for first side of back opening.

Next row Cast on 3 sts, moss st these 3 sts, then moss
st to end.

Cont in moss st until back measures 33(38:46:52)cm
from cast on edge, ending with a wrong side row.

Shape neck

Next row Moss st to last 6(8:8:10) sts, leave these sts
on a holder, turn.

Dec one st at neck edge on every row until 5(7:9:11)
sts rem.

Cont straight until back measures 36(41:49:55)cm
from cast on edge, ending with a wrong side row.

Shape shoulder

Cast off.

With right side facing, rejoin yarn to rem sts, moss st
to end.

Cont in moss st until back measures 33(38:46:52)cm
from cast on edge, ending with a wrong side row.

Shape neck

Next row Moss st 6(8:8:10) sts, leave these sts on a
holder, moss st to end.

Dec one st at neck edge on every row until 5(7:9:11)
sts rem.

Cont straight until back measures 36(41:49:55)cm
from cast on edge, ending with a wrong side row.

Shape shoulder

Cast off.

DRESS FRONT

Work as given for Back from ** to **.

Shape neck

Next row (right side) Moss st 11(13:15:17) sts, turn
and work on these sts for first side of neck shaping.

Dec 1 st at neck edge on every foll alt row until
5(7:9:11) sts rem.

Cont without further shaping until front measures
same as Back to shoulder, ending at side edge.

picot dress and bag

Shape shoulder

Cast off.

With right side facing, slip centre 9(11:13:15) sts onto a holder, rejoin yarn to rem sts, moss st to end. Complete to match first side, reversing shaping.

NECKBAND

Join shoulder seams.

With right side facing and 2¾mm circular knitting needle, slip 6(8:8:10) sts from left back onto needle, pick up and k11 sts up left back to shoulder, 18(20:22:24) sts down left front neck, k across 9(11:13:15) sts from front neck holder, pick up and k18(20:22:24) sts up right front neck to shoulder, 11 sts from right back neck, k across 6(8:8:10) sts on back neck holder. 79(89:95:105) sts.

Work backwards and forwards in rows.

K 1 row.

Buttonhole row K1, yf, k2tog, k to end.

Picot cast off row (wrong side) Working knitwise, cast off 5, * slip st from right needle back onto left needle, cast on 2 sts, cast off 5; rep from * ending last repeat: cast off rem sts.

ARMBANDS

Join left shoulder and neckband seam.

With right side facing and 2¾mm knitting needles, pick up and k66(72:78:84) sts evenly around armhole edge.

K 2 rows.

Picot cast off row (wrong side) Working knitwise, cast off 12, [sl st from right needle back onto left needle, cast on 2 sts, cast off 5 sts] 15(17:19:21) times, cast off rem sts.

POCKET

With 3¼mm needles, cast on 11 sts.

1st row K1, [p1, k1] to end.

2nd row As 1st row.

3rd row Pk, [p1, k1] to last 2 sts, p1, kp.

4th row P1, [k1, p1] to end.

5th row Kp, [k1, p1] to last 2 sts, k1, pk.

6th row K1, [p1, k1] to end.

Rep the last 4 rows 4 times more. 31 sts.

Work 6th row twice more.

Eyelet row (right side) K1, [p2tog, yo, p1, k2tog, yf, k1] twice, p2tog, yo, p1, yo, p2tog, [k1, yf, k2tog, p1, yo, p2tog] twice, k1.

Next row K1, [p1, k1] to end.

Picot cast off row (right side) Cast off 3, * sl st from right needle back onto left needle, cast on 2 sts, cast off 5 sts; rep from * to end.

TO FINISH

Join side and armband seams. Lap buttonband behind buttonhole band and catch in place. Sew on button. Cut ribbon in half and stitch one end of each length to wrong side of eyelet row ends of pocket. Thread ribbons through eyelets, pull up and tie at centre front. Position pocket on dress front and slipstitch in place.

NOTE

The bag is worked in one piece starting at the centre of the base.

TO MAKE

With 3¼mm needles, cast on 8 sts.

1st row (right side) [Kfb] to end. 16 sts.

P 1 row.

3rd row [Kfb] to last st, k1. 31 sts.

P 1 row.

5th row [K4, kfb] 6 times, k1. 37 sts.

P 1 row.

7th row [K5, kfb] 6 times, k1. 43 sts.

Cont to inc 6 sts on foll 4 right side rows, working 1 st more between incs on every inc row. 67 sts.

Next row (wrong side) K.

Next row K.

Moss st row P1, [k1, p1] to end.

Rep the last row 3 times more.

Next row (wrong side) * P3, [k1, p1] twice, k1; rep from * to last 3 sts, p3.

Next row * K4, [p1, k1] twice; rep from * to last 3 sts, k3.

Next row [P5, k1, p2] to last 3 sts, p3.

Beg with a k row, work 21 rows in st st.

Next row (wrong side) [P5, k1, p2] to last 3 sts, p3.

Next row * K4, [p1, k1] twice; rep from * to last 3 sts, k3.

Next row * P3, [k1, p1] twice, k1; rep from * to last 3 sts, p3.

Next row P1, [k1, p1] to end.

Rep the last row 3 times more.

K 1 row.

P 1 row.

Eyelet row (right side) K1, [k2, yf, k2tog] 8 times, k2, [k2tog tbl, yf, k2] 8 times.

P 1 row.

Next row P1, [k1, p1] to end.

Rep the last row 4 times more.

Picot cast off row (wrong side) Cast off 3, * slip st on right needle back onto left needle, cast on 2 sts, cast off 5 sts; rep from * to end.

TO FINISH

Join centre back seam and continue seam to form the base. Thread a large-eyed needle with narrow ribbon and beginning with eyelet hole to the left of the centre front, thread ribbon through the eyelets twice, so ending with ribbon coming to the right side through the eyelet to the right of centre front. Tie the ribbon into a bow at centre front and pull one of the loops running between the eyelets of the centre back to gather the bag and form a hanging loop.

picot dress and bag

velvet-edged jacket

MEASUREMENTS

To fit ages	0–3	3–6	6–9	9–12	12–24	months

ACTUAL MEASUREMENTS

Chest	48	52	56	60	65	cm
Length to shoulder	21	24	26	28	32	cm
Sleeve length	13	15	17	19	22	cm

MATERIALS

- 2(3:3:4:4) 50g balls of Debbie Bliss baby cashmerino in Pale Blue
- Pair each of 3mm and 3¼mm knitting needles
- 1m narrow piped ribbon for edging
- 6(6:6:6:7) buttons

TENSION

25 sts and 34 rows to 10cm square over st st using 3¼mm needles.

ABBREVIATIONS

See page 121.

BACK

With 3mm needles, cast on 62(66:70:74:82) sts.
K 3 rows.
Change to 3¼mm needles.
Beg with a k row, work in st st until back measures 12(14:15:16:18)cm from cast on edge, ending with a p row.

Shape armholes

Cast off 3(3:3:3:4) sts at beg of next 2 rows.
Dec one st at each end of the next and 3(3:3:3:4) foll alt rows. 48(52:56:60:64) sts.
Cont in st st until back measures 21(24:26:28:32)cm from cast on edge, ending with a p row.

Shape shoulders

Cast off 13(14:15:16:17) sts at beg of next 2 rows.
Cast off rem 22(24:26:28:30) sts.

LEFT FRONT

With 3mm needles, cast on 31(33:35:37:41) sts.
K 3 rows.
Change to 3¼mm needles.
Beg with a k row, work in st st until front measures 12(14:15:16:18)cm from cast on edge, ending with a p row.

Shape armhole

Cast off 3(3:3:3:4) sts at beg of next row.
Work 1 row.
Dec one st at beg of the next and 3(3:3:3:4) foll alt rows. 24(26:28:30:32) sts.
Cont in st st until front measures 17(19:21:22:26)cm from cast on edge, ending with a p row.

Shape neck

Next row K to last 4(5:5:5:6) sts, leave these sts on a holder.
Dec one st at neck edge on every row until 13(14:15:16:17) sts rem.
Cont straight until front measures same as Back to shoulder, ending at armhole edge.

Shape shoulder

Cast off.

velvet-edged jacket

RIGHT FRONT

With 3mm needles, cast on 31(33:35:37:41) sts.

K 3 rows.

Change to 3¼mm needles.

Beg with a k row, work in st st until front measures 12(14:15:16:18)cm from cast on edge, ending with a k row.

Shape armhole

Cast off 3(3:3:3:4) sts at beg of next row.

Dec one st at end of the next and 3(3:3:3:4) foll alt rows. 24(26:28:30:32) sts.

Cont in st st until front measures 17(19:21:22:26)cm from cast on edge, ending with a p row.

Shape neck

Next row K4(5:5:5:6) sts, leave these sts on a holder, k to end.

Dec one st at neck edge on every row until 13(14:15:16:17) sts rem.

Cont straight until front measures same as Back to shoulder, ending at armhole edge.

Shape shoulder

Cast off.

SLEEVES

With 3mm needles, cast on 32(34:38:40:44) sts.

K 3 rows.

Change to 3¼mm needles.

Beg with a k row, work in st st and inc one st at each end of the 3rd and every foll 4th row until there are 50(54:60:66:74) sts.

Cont straight until sleeve measures 13(15:17:19:22)cm from cast on edge, ending with a p row.

Cast off 3(3:3:3:4) sts at beg of next 2 rows.

Dec one st at each end of the next and 3(3:3:3:4) foll alt rows. 36(40:46:52:56) sts.

Cast off.

BUTTON BAND

With right side facing and 3mm needles, leaving a long yarn end, pick up and k46(51:58:63:69) sts along left front edge.

K 4 rows.

Cast off.

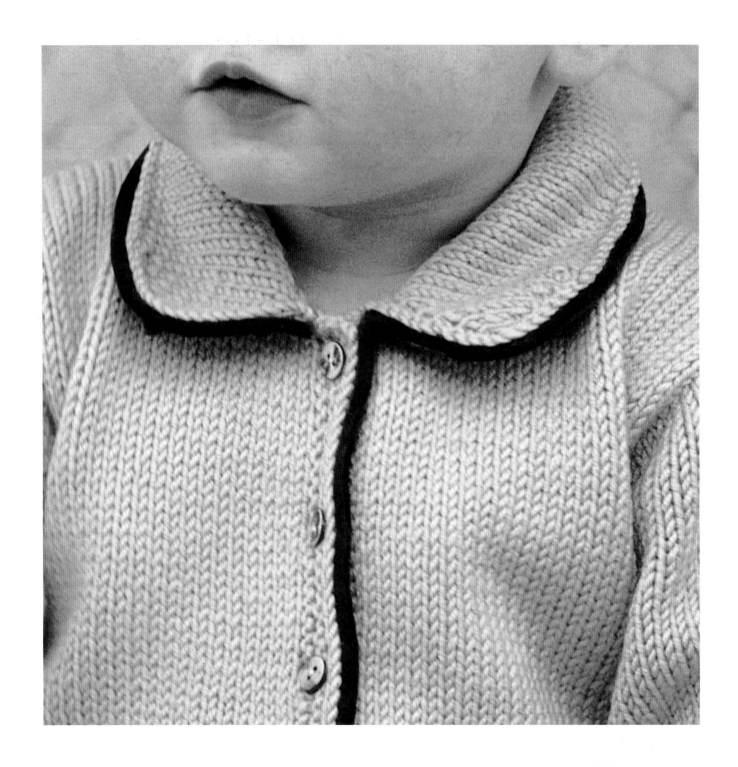

BUTTONHOLE BAND

With right side facing and 3mm needles, pick up and k46(51:58:63:69) sts along right front edge.
K 1 row.
Buttonhole row (right side) K2(2:3:3:4), [k2tog, yf, k6(7:8:9:8) sts] 5(5:5:5:6) times, k2tog, yf, k2(2:3:3:3).
K 1 row.
Cast off.

COLLAR

Join shoulder seams.
With right side facing and 3¼mm needles, slip 4(5:5:5:6) sts on right front holder onto a needle, pick up and k16(16:17:18:18) sts up right front neck, 22(24:26:28:30) sts from back neck and 16(16:17:18:18) sts down left front neck, then k4(5:5:5:6) sts from left front holder.
62(66:70:74:78) sts.
Beg with a k row work in st st, shaping as folls:
Next 2 rows Work to last 20(21:22:23:24) sts, turn.
Next 2 rows Work to last 14(15:16:17:18) sts, turn.
Next 2 rows Work to last 8(9:10:11:12) sts, turn.
Next row K all sts.
Next row P all sts.
Next row K1, m1, k to last st, m1, k1.
Next row P to end.
Rep the last 2 rows 3(4:4:5:5) times more.
70(76:80:86:90) sts.

Next row Skpo, k to last 2 sts, k2tog.
Next row P2tog, p to last 2 sts, p2tog tbl.
Rep the last 2 rows 1(2:2:3:3) times more.
With right side of collar facing, 3¼mm needle and long yarn end from button band, pick up and k14(18:18:22:22) sts along row ends of collar, then using main ball of yarn k across 62(64:68:70:74) sts of collar, then pick up and k14(18:18:22:22) sts along row ends of collar. 90(100:104:114:118) sts.
Cast off knitwise.

TO FINISH

With centre of cast off edge of sleeve to shoulder, sew sleeves into armholes. Join side and sleeve seams. Sew fabric edge of piped edging under the outside edge of collar, behind the buttonhole band and lower sleeve edges. Sew on buttons.

velvet-edged jacket

fair isle top

MEASUREMENTS

To fit ages		6–12		12–18	18–24		months

ACTUAL MEASUREMENTS

Chest		52		56		61		cm
Length to shoulder		28		32		36		cm
Sleeve length		18		21		24		cm

MATERIALS

- 3(3:4) 50g balls Debbie Bliss baby cashmerino in Pale Blue (A).
- Small amounts of Mallard (B), Lime Green (C), Rose (D), Pale Pink (E) and White (F)
- Pair 3¼mm knitting needles
- 3¼mm circular knitting needle
- 2 small buttons
- 14 small blue beads and 40 small pink beads
- Sewing thread

TENSION

25 sts and 34 rows to 10cm square over st st using 3¼mm needles.

ABBREVIATIONS

See page 121.

CHART NOTE

When working from charts, read right side (k) rows from right to left and wrong side (p) rows from left to right. Strand yarn not in use loosely across wrong side of work to keep fabric elastic.

BACK

With 3¼mm needles and B, cast on 67(73:79) sts.
Beg with a k row, work 3 rows in st st.
Picot row P1, * yrn, p2tog; rep from * to end.
Change to C .
Work 2 rows in st st.
Change to A.
Cont in st st and work 6 rows.
Beg with a k row, work 13 rows in st st from chart 1, working between lines for correct size and repeating the 16 st patt rep.
Cont in A until back measures 17(20:23)cm from picot row, ending with a p row.
Shape armholes
Cast off 7(8:9) sts at beg of next 2 rows. 53(57:61) sts.
Cont straight until back measures 21(24:27)cm from picot row, ending with a p row.

Back opening

Next row K25(27:29) sts, turn and work on these sts for first side of back opening, leave rem sts on a spare needle.
Next row Cast on 3 sts, k these sts, then p to end. 28(30:32) sts.
Next row K to end.
Next row K3, p to end.
Rep the last 2 rows until back measures 28(32:36)cm from picot row, ending at armhole edge.
Shape shoulder
Next row Cast off 12(13:14) sts, k to end.
Next row K3, p to end.
Leave these 16(17:18) sts on a holder.
With right side facing, rejoin yarn to rem sts on spare needle, k to end.
Next row P to last 3 sts, k3.
Next row K to end.
Rep the last 2 rows until back measures 25(28:31)cm from picot row, ending with a wrong side row.
Buttonhole row K1, k2tog, yf, k to end.
Work straight until back measures 28(32:36)cm from picot row, ending at armhole edge.
Shape shoulder
Next row Cast off 12(13:14) sts, p to last 3 sts, k3.
Leave these 16(17:18) sts on a holder.

fair isle top

FRONT

Work as given for Back until front measures 23(26:30)cm from picot row, ending with a p row.

Shape neck

Next row K19(20:21) sts, turn and work on these sts for first side of neck shaping, leave rem sts on a spare needle.

Dec 1 st at neck edge on every foll alt row until 12(13:14) sts rem.

Cont without further shaping until front measures same as Back to shoulder, ending at side edge.

Shape shoulder

Cast off.

With right side facing, slip centre 15(17:19) sts onto a holder, rejoin yarn to rem sts, k to end.

Complete to match first side, reversing shaping.

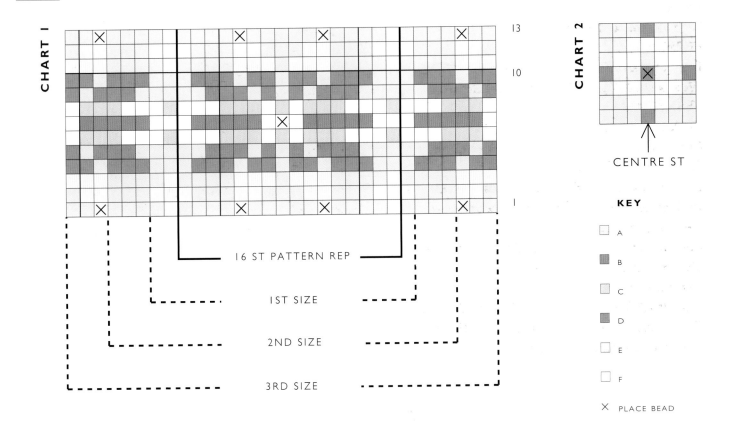

CHART 1

13

10

1

16 ST PATTERN REP

1ST SIZE

2ND SIZE

3RD SIZE

CHART 2

CENTRE ST

KEY

☐ A

▨ B

☐ C

▧ D

☐ E

☐ F

✕ PLACE BEAD

SLEEVES

With 3¼mm needles and B, cast on
49(55:61) sts.
Beg with a k row, work 3 rows in st st.
Picot row P1, * yrn, p2tog; rep from * to end.
Beg with a k row, work in st st throughout.
Change to C and work 2 rows.
Change to A and work 4 rows.
Work 7 rows in st st from chart 2, placing centre st of
chart on centre st of row.
Cont in A only.
Next row P to end and inc 1 st in centre of row.
50(56:62) sts.
Dec row K3, skpo, k to last 5 sts, k2tog, k3.
Work 5 rows in st st.
Rep the last 6 rows 3(4:5) times more and the dec row
again. 40(44:48) sts.
Work 3 rows in st st.
Inc row K3, m1, k to last 3 sts, m1, k3.
Rep the last 4 rows 4(5:6) times more. 50(56:62) sts.
Cont straight until sleeve measures 18(21:24)cm from
picot row, ending with a p row.
Mark each end of last row with a coloured thread.
Work a further 6(8:8) rows.
Cast off.

NECKBAND

Join shoulder seams.
With right side facing, 3¼mm circular needle and A,
work k1, k2tog, yf, k13(14:15) from sts on left back
holder, pick up and k20(20:21) sts down left front
neck, k across 15(17:19) sts from front neck holder,
pick up and k20(20:21) sts up right front neck to
shoulder, then k across 16(17:18) sts from right back
holder. 87(91:97) sts.
Cut yarn.
Change to E and keeping right side facing, k 1 row.
Now work back and forth in rows.
Next row (wrong side) Cast off 3 sts, p to last 3 sts,
cast off these 3 sts.
Change to D.
K 1 row.
Picot row (wrong side) P1, * yrn, p2tog; rep from *
to end.
Work 2 rows in st st.
Cast off.

TO FINISH

With centre of cast off edge of sleeve to shoulder, sew
sleeves into armholes with row ends above markers
sewn to cast off sts at underarm. Join side and sleeve
seams. Fold edges onto wrong side along picot row
and slipstitch in place. Sew on buttons.

BEADS

Sew beads onto the garment where indicated on the
charts, omitting beads where they would be
incorporated into the side or sleeve seams.

fair isle top

bow-tied bolero

MEASUREMENTS

To fit ages		6–9	9–12	12–18	18–24	24–36	months

ACTUAL MEASUREMENTS

Chest		48	51	54	57	64	cm
Length to shoulder		17	19	21	23	25	cm
Sleeve length		9	11	12	14	16	cm

MATERIALS

• 2(3:3:4:4) 50g balls of Debbie Bliss baby cashmerino in Rose
• Pair each of 3mm and 3¼mm knitting needles
• Circular 3mm knitting needle

TENSION

25 sts and 34 rows to 10cm square over st st using
3¼mm needles.

ABBREVIATIONS

See page 121.

BACK

With 3mm needles, cast on 62(66:70:74:82) sts.

K 3 rows.

Change to 3¼mm needles.

Beg with a k row, work 24(26:28:30:32) rows in st st.

Shape armholes

Cast off 3(3:3:3:4) sts at beg of next 2 rows.

Dec one st at each end of the next and 3(3:3:3:4) foll alt rows. 48(52:56:60:64) sts.

Cont in st st until back measures 17(19:21:23:25)cm from cast on edge, ending with a p row.

Shape shoulders

Cast off 13(14:15:16:17) sts at beg of next 2 rows.

Leave rem 22(24:26:28:30) sts on a holder.

LEFT FRONT

With 3mm needles, cast on 93(99:105:111:123) sts.

K 3 rows.

Change to 3¼mm needles.

Next row K to last 3 sts, m1, k3.

Next row K3, p to end.

Rep the last 2 rows 2(3:4:5:6) times more. 96(103:110:117:130) sts.

Next row K to last 32(37:42:47:56) sts, turn and leave these sts on a holder.

Next row Sl 1, p to end.

Next row K to last 10 sts, turn and leave these sts on a holder.

Next row Sl 1, p to end.

Next row K to last 8 sts, turn and leave these sts on a holder.

Next row Sl 1, p to end.

Next row K to last 6 sts, turn and leave these sts on a holder.

Next row Sl 1, p to end.

Next row K to last 4 sts, turn and leave these sts on a holder.

Next row Sl 1, p to end.

Next row K to last 2 sts, turn and leave these sts on a holder.

Next row Sl 1, p to end.

Next row K to last 2 sts, k2tog.

Next row P2tog, p to end.

Rep the last 2 rows twice more. 28(30:32:34:38) sts.

Shape armhole

Next row Cast off 3(3:3:3:4) sts, k to last 2 sts, k2tog.

Next row P to end.

Next row Skpo, k to last 2 sts, k2tog.

Next row P to end.

Rep the last 2 rows 3(3:3:3:4) times.

Keeping armhole edge straight, cont to dec at neck edge on every foll 4th row until 13(14:15:16:17) sts rem.

Cont straight until front measures same as Back to shoulder, ending at armhole edge.

Shape shoulder

Cast off.

RIGHT FRONT

With 3mm needles, cast on 93(99:105:111:123) sts.

K 3 rows.

Change to 3¼mm needles.

Next row K3, m1, k to end.

Next row P to last 3 sts, k3.

bow-tied bolero

Rep the last 2 rows 2(3:4:5:6) times more.
96(103:110:117:130) sts.
Next row K32(37:42:47:56) sts, leave these sts on a holder, k to end.
Next row P to last st, sl 1.
Next row K10 sts, leave these sts on a holder, k to end.
Next row P to last st, sl 1.
Next row K8 sts, leave these sts on a holder, k to end.
Next row P to last st, sl 1.
Next row K6 sts, leave these sts on a holder, k to end.
Next row P to last st, sl 1.
Next row K4 sts, leave these sts on a holder, k to end.
Next row P to last st, sl 1.
Next row K2 sts, leave these sts on a holder, k to end.
Next row P to last st, sl 1.
Next row Skpo, k to end.
Next row P to last 2 sts, p2tog tbl.
Rep the last 2 rows twice more.
Next row Skpo, k to end. 27(29:31:33:37) sts.
Shape armhole
Next row Cast off 3(3:3:3:4) sts, p to end.
Next row Skpo, k to last 2 sts, k2tog.
Next row P to end.
Rep the last 2 rows 3(3:3:3:4) times.
Keeping armhole edge straight, cont to dec at neck edge on every foll 4th row until 13(14:15:16:17) sts rem.
Cont straight until front measures same as Back to shoulder, ending at armhole edge.
Shape shoulder
Cast off.

SLEEVES
With 3mm needles, cast on 38(40:44:48:52) sts.
K 3 rows.
Change to 3¼mm needles.
Beg with a k row, work in st st and inc one st at each end of the 3rd and every foll 4th row until there are 50(54:60:66:74) sts.
Cont straight until sleeve measures 9(11:12:14:16)cm from cast on edge, ending with a p row.
Cast off 3(3:3:3:4) sts at beg of next 2 rows.
Dec one st at each end of the next and 3(3:3:3:4) foll alt rows. 36(40:46:52:56) sts.
Cast off.

FRONT EDGING
Join shoulder seams.
With right side facing and 3mm circular needle, slip 62(67:72:77:86) sts from right front holders onto needle, pick up and k27(30:33:36:40) sts up right front to shoulder, k across 22(24:26:28:30) sts at back neck, pick up and k27(30:33:36:40) sts down left front, then k across 62(67:72:77:86) sts on left front holders. 200(218:236:254:282) sts.
Working backwards and forwards, k 3 rows.
Cast off.

TO FINISH
Sew sleeves into armholes. Join side and sleeve seams.

beaded cardigan

MEASUREMENTS

To fit ages		12–18	18–24	24–36	months

ACTUAL MEASUREMENTS

Chest		63	66	69	cm
Length to shoulder		28	32	36	cm
Sleeve length		19	22	24	cm

MATERIALS

- 4(4:5) 50g balls of Debbie Bliss baby cashmerino in Pale Blue
- Pair each of 3mm and 3¼mm knitting needles
- 7(7:8) buttons
- Approximately 25(30:35)g small glass beads with a silver core

25 sts and 34 rows to 10cm square over st st using
3¼mm needles.

ABBREVIATIONS
See page 121.

BACK
With 3¼mm needles, cast on 81(85:89) sts.
Moss st row K1, * p1, k1; rep from * to end.
This row forms moss st.
Rep the last row 3 times more.
5th row (right side) [K1, p1] 2(3:4) times, * k3, p1,
[k1, p1] 3 times; rep from * to last 7(9:11) sts, k3,
[p1, k1] 2(3:4) times.
6th row P0(0:2), [k1, p1] 1(2:2) times, k1, * p5, k1,
[p1, k1] twice; rep from * to last 8(10:12) sts, p5, k1,
[p1, k1] 1(2:2) times, p0(0:2).
7th row K1(1:3), p1, k0(1:1), p0(1:1), k7, * p1, k1, p1,
k7; rep from * to last 2(4:6) sts, p1, k1, p0(1:1),
k0(1:3).
8th row P0(2:4), * k1, p9; rep from * to last 1(3:5) sts,
k1, p0(2:4).
9th row K.
10th row P.
11th row K0(2:4), * p1, k9; rep from * to last 1(3:5)
sts, p1, k0(2:4).

12th row P1(1:3), *k1, p1, k1, p7; rep from * to last
2(4:6) sts, [k1, p1] 1(2:2) times, p0(0:2).
13th row As 11th row.
14th row P.
15th row K5(7:9), * p1, k9; rep from * to last 6(8:10)
sts, p1, k5(7:9).
16th row P4(6:8), * k1, p1, k1, p7; rep from * to last
7(9:11) sts, k1, p1, k1, p4(6:8).
17th row As 15th row.
The last 8 rows (10th to 17th patt rows) form the patt
and are repeated.
Cont in patt until back measures 28(32:36)cm from
cast on edge, ending with a wrong side row.
Shape shoulders
Cast off 23(24:25) sts at beg of next 2 rows.
Leave rem 35(37:39) sts on a spare needle.

beaded cardigan

LEFT FRONT

With 3¼mm needles, cast on 43(45:47) sts.

Moss st row K1, * p1, k1; rep from * to end.

Rep the last row 3 times more.

5th row (right side) [K1, p1] 2(3:4) times, * k3, p1, [k1, p1] 3 times; rep from * to last 9 sts, k3, [p1, k1] 3 times.

6th row K1, [p1, k1] twice, * p5, k1, [p1, k1] twice; rep from * to last 8(10:12) sts, p5, k1, [p1, k1] 1(2:2) times, p0(0:2).

7th row K1(1:3), p1, k0(1:1), p0(1:1), k7, * p1, k1, p1, k7; rep from * to last 4 sts, [p1, k1] twice.

8th row K1, p1, * k1, p9; rep from * to last 1(3:5) sts, k1, p0(2:4).

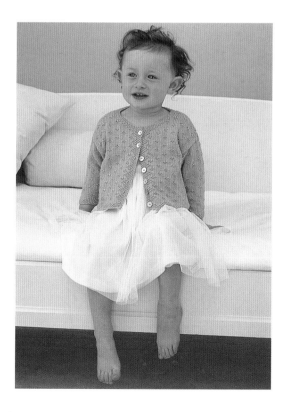

9th row K to last 4 sts, [p1, k1] twice.

10th row K1, [p1, k1] twice, p to end.

11th row K0(2:4), * p1, k9; rep from * to last 13 sts, p1, k6, [p1, k1] 3 times.

12th row K1, [p1, k1] 3 times, p4, * k1, p1, k1, p7; rep from * to last 2(4:6) sts, [k1, p1] 1(2:2) times, p0(0:2).

13th row As 11th row.

14th row As 10th row.

15th row K5(7:9), * p1, k9; rep from * to last 8 sts, p1, k3, [p1, k1] twice.

16th row K1, p1, k1, p3, * k1, p1, k1, p7; rep from * to last 7(9:11) sts, k1, p1, k1, p4(6:8).

17th row As 15th row.

The last 8 rows (10th to 17th patt rows) form the patt and are repeated.

Cont in patt until left front measures 21(25:29)cm from cast on edge, ending with a wrong side row.

Shape neck

Next row Patt to last 8(9:10) sts, leave these sts on a holder.

Dec one st at neck edge on every row until 23(24:25) sts rem.

Cont straight until front measures same as Back to shoulder, ending at armhole edge.

Shape shoulder

Cast off.

Mark the position for 7(7:8) buttons, the first to come on the 5th row, the last just below the neck shaping, with the rem 5(5:6) evenly spaced between.

RIGHT FRONT

With 3¼mm needles, cast on 43(45:47) sts.

Moss st row K1, * p1, k1; rep from * to end.

Rep the last row 3 times more.

Next row (buttonhole row) K1, p1, yon, p2tog, k1, p1, * k3, p1, [k1, p1] 3 times; rep from * to last 7(9:11) sts, k3, [p1, k1] 2(3:4) times.

6th row P0(0:2), [k1, p1] 1(2:2) times, k1, * p5, k1, [p1, k1] twice; rep from * to end.

7th row [K1, p1] twice, k7, * p1, k1, p1, k7; rep from * to last 2(4:6) sts, p1, k1, p0(1:1), k0(1:3).

8th row P0(2:4), * k1, p9; rep from * to last 3 sts, k1, p1, k1.

9th row [K1, p1] twice, k to end.

10th row P to last 5 sts, [k1, p1] twice, k1.

11th row [K1, p1] 3 times, k6, * p1, k9; rep from * to last 1(3:5) sts, p1, k0(2:4).

12th row P0(0:3), [p1, k1] 1(2:2) times, * p7, k1, p1, k1; rep from * to last 11 sts, p4, k1, [p1, k1] 3 times.

13th row As 11th row.

14th row As 10th row.

15th row [K1, p1] twice, k3, * p1, k9; rep from * to last 6(8:10) sts, p1, k5(7:9).

16th row P4(6:8), * k1, p1, k1, p7; rep from * to last 9 sts, k1, p1, k1, p3, k1, p1, k1.

17th row As 15th row.

The last 8 rows (10th to 17th patt rows) form the patt and are repeated.

Cont in patt working buttonholes on right side rows to match button markers, until right front measures 21(25:29)cm from cast on edge, ending with the same wrong side row as left front.

Shape neck

Next row Patt 8(9:10) sts, slip these sts onto a holder, patt to end.

Dec one st at neck edge on every row until 23(24:25) sts rem.

Cont straight until front measures same as Back to shoulder, ending at armhole edge.

Shape shoulder

Cast off.

beaded cardigan

SLEEVES

With 3¼mm needles, cast on 35(37:39) sts.

1st and 3rd sizes only

Moss st row P1, * k1, p1; rep from * to end.

Rep the last row 3 times more.

2nd size only

Moss st row K1, * p1, k1; rep from * to end.

Rep the last row 3 times more.

All sizes

5th row (right side) P0(0:1), k0(1:1), p1, k3, * p1, [k1, p1] 3 times, k3; rep from * to last 1(2:3) sts, p1, k0(1:1), p0(0:1).

6th row P0(0:1), k0(1:1), p5, * k1, [p1, k1] twice, p5; rep from * to last 0(1:2) sts, k0(1:1), p0(0:1).

7th row P0(0:1), k6(7:7), * p1, k1, p1, k7; rep from * to last 9(10:11) sts, p1, k1, p1, k6(7:7), p0(0:1).

8th row P7(8:9), k1, * p9, k1; rep from * to last 7(8:9) sts, k7(8:9).

9th row K1, m1, k to last st, m1, k1.

10th row P.

11th row K8(9:10), * p1, k9; rep from * to last 9(10:11) sts, p1, k8(9:10).

12th row P7(8:9), * k1, p1, k1, p7; rep from * to last 0(1:2)sts, p0(1:2).

13th row K1, m1, k7(8:9), * p1, k9; rep from * to last 9(10:11) sts, p1, k7(8:9), m1, k1.

14th row P.

15th row K4(5:6), * p1, k9; rep from * to last 5(6:7) sts, p1, k4(5:6).

16th row P3(4:5), * k1, p1, k1, p7; rep from * to last 6(7:8) sts, k1, p1, k1, p3(4:5).

17th row K1, m1, k3(4:5), * p1, k9; rep from * to last 5(6:7) sts, p1, k3(4:5), m1, k1.

The last 8 rows set the position of the patt, cont in patt and inc one st at each end of every foll 4th row until there are 63(71:79) sts, taking all inc sts into patt.

Cont straight until sleeve measures 19(22:24)cm from cast on edge, ending with a wrong side row.

Cast off.

NECKBAND

Join shoulder seams.

With right side facing and 3mm needles, slip 8(9:10) sts from right front neck holder onto a needle, pick up and k20 sts up right front neck, k35(37:39) sts from back neck holder, pick up and k20 sts down left front neck, patt across 8(9:10) sts from left front neck holder. 91(95:99) sts.

Work 5 rows in moss st.

Cast off in moss st.

TO FINISH

Matching centre of cast off edge of sleeve to shoulder, sew on sleeves. Stitch one bead to the centre of each tiny diamond, omitting diamonds that will be incorporated into the side and sleeve seams. Join side and sleeve seams. Sew on buttons.

sampler blanket

MEASUREMENTS

Approximately 24½ x 30in

MATERIALS

Six 1¾oz (50g) balls of Debbie Bliss baby cashmerino in White (A)
One 1¾oz (50g) ball in each of Indigo (B), Duck Egg (C) and Wedgwood (D)
Pair of US 3 (3¼mm) knitting needles
Large-eyed, blunt-pointed embroidery needle

TENSION

25 sts and 34 rows to 10cm square over st st using
3¼mm needles.

ABBREVIATIONS

See page 121.

CHART NOTES

To work from chart read 1st and every right side (k) row from right to left, 2nd and every wrong side (p) row from left to right.

Use separate lengths of yarn for each motif and wherever possible for the background in A between motifs. Twist yarns when changing colours to link areas. Work the area within the dotted outline containing the letters and numbers in plain stocking stitch. Cross stitch the alphabet or use the letters and numbers to work a name and date after completing the knitting.

TO MAKE

With 3¼mm needles and A, cast on 157 sts.

1st row (right side) P1, [k1, p1] to end.

2nd row K1, [p1, k1] to end.

3rd row K1, [p1, k1] to end.

4th row P1, [k1, p1] to end.

These 4 rows form double moss st.

Work 7 more rows, so ending with a right side row.

Next row (wrong side) Double moss st 11, k to last 11 sts, double moss st 11.

This row forms a ridge on the right side to outline the lower edge of the pattern area.

Next row (right side) Double moss st 11, p1, k133, p1, double moss st 11.

Next row Double moss st 11, k1, p133, k1, double moss st 11.

These 2 rows form st st with a single st in reverse st st and 11 sts in double moss st at each side.

Work 4 more rows.

Now work in patt from chart as folls:

1st row (right side) With A, patt 15, k127 sts of 1st row of chart, with A, patt 15.

2nd row With A, patt 15, p127 sts of 2nd row of chart, with A, patt 15.

These 2 rows set the position of the chart with 11 sts in double moss st and 4 sts in st st in A, worked at each side.

Cont in patt as set until all 227 chart rows have been worked.

Cont in A only.

Next row (wrong side) Double moss st 11, k1, p133, k1, double moss st 11.

Working centre 133 sts in st st, work 4 more rows.

Next row (right side) Double moss st 11, p135, double moss st 11.

This last row forms a ridge to outline the top edge of the pattern area.

Work 10 rows in double moss st.

Cast off knitwise.

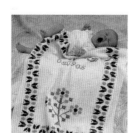

sampler blanket

WORKING THE CROSS STITCH

The letters and numbers shown on the chart fit into
an area 69 stitches by 106 rows. To work the complete
alphabet as shown, use tacking thread to outline the
stitches and rows indicated by the dotted line on the
chart, then tack a base line for each row of letters. Use
a blunt-pointed needle and work the cross stitch from
the chart, placing each cross stitch over a knitted
stitch, taking care to make all the top diagonals of the
cross stitches lie in the same direction.

To cross stitch a name and date, plan your design on
graph paper. The maximum area that lettering can
comfortably be fitted into is 79 stitches by 110 rows.
Mark this area on graph paper, then draw in dotted
lines horizontally and vertically to cross at the centre.
Place an equal amount of letters at each side of the
centre vertical line and aim for no more than five or
six letters on each line, with a maximum of six lines.
Plan the lettering on the graph paper, adjusting the
space between letters as necessary. Mark out the area
to be worked on the blanket with tacking stitches, and
tack guide lines for each row of letters and numbers
before working the cross stitch from your chart.

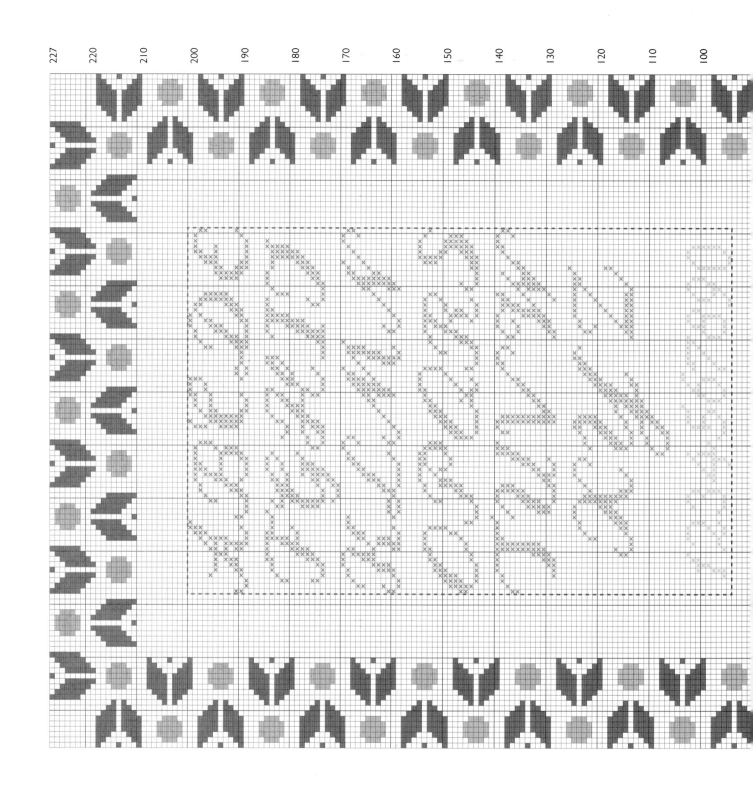

sampler blanket

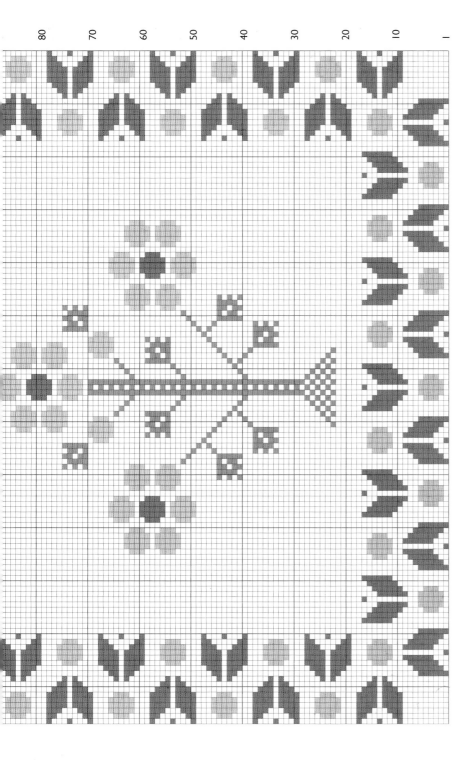

KEY

- ☐ A
- ▨ B
- ▨ C
- ▨ D

✕ CROSS STITCH IN C
ON COMPLETION

✕ CROSS STITCH IN D
ON COMPLETION

80 70 60 50 40 30 20 10 1

organza-edged cardigan

MEASUREMENTS

| To fit ages | 3–6 | 6–9 | 9–12 | 12–24 | months |

ACTUAL MEASUREMENTS

Chest	51	55	60	64	cm
Length to shoulder	26	28	34	37	cm
Sleeve length	15	17	19	22	cm

MATERIALS

- 3(3:4:4) 50g balls of Debbie Bliss cotton cashmere double knitting in Grape
- Pair each of 3¼mm and 3¾mm knitting needles
- Approximately 1.5m organza ribbon

ABBREVIATONS

See page 121.

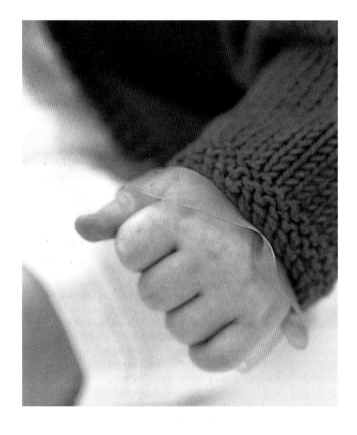

BACK AND FRONTS

With 3¼mm needles, cast on 59(63:69:73) sts.

K 3 rows.

Change to 3¾mm needles.

Beg with a k row, work in st st until back measures
25(27:33:36)cm from cast on edge, ending with
a k row.

Next row P15(17:19:21), k29(29:31:31),
p15(17:19:21).

Next row K to end.

Next row P15(17:19:21), k29(29:31:31), p15(17:19:21).

Divide for fronts

Mark each end of last row with a coloured thread.

Next row K17(19:21:23), turn and work on these sts
for right front, leave rem sts on a spare needle.

Next row K3, p to end.

Next row K to end.

Rep the last 2 rows once more and the first row again.

Next row K to last 3 sts, m1, k3.

Next row K3, p to end.

Next row K to end.

Next row K3, m1 purlwise, p to end.

Next row K to end.

Next row K3, p to end.

Cont in this way increasing one st inside garter st border
on every 3rd row until there are 25(27:30:32) sts.

Keeping 3 sts at front edge in garter st work straight
until the same number of rows have been worked in st
st as on Back to markers, ending with a p row.

Change to 3¼mm needles.

P 3 rows.

Cast off purlwise.

With right side facing, rejoin yarn to rem sts on spare
needle, cast off next 25(25:27:27) sts, k to end.

Next row P to last 3 sts, k3.

Next row K to end.

Rep the last 2 rows once more and the first row again.

Next row K3, m1, k to end.

organza-edged cardigan

Next row P to last 3 sts, k3.
Next row K to end.
Next row P to last 3 sts, m1 purlwise, k3.
Next row K to end.
Next row P to last 3 sts, k3.
Cont in this way increasing one st inside garter st border on every 3rd row until there are 25(27:30:32) sts.
Keeping 3 sts at front edge in garter st work straight until the same number of rows have been worked in st st as on back to markers, ending with a p row.
Change to 3¼mm needles.
P 3 rows.
Cast off purlwise.

SLEEVES

With 3¼mm needles, cast on 35(37:39:43) sts.
K 3 rows.
Change to 3¾mm needles.
Beg with a k row, work in st st, inc one st at each end of the 7th and every foll 4th row until there are 49(53:59:65) sts.
Cont straight until sleeve measures 15(17:19:22)cm from cast on edge, ending with a wrong side row.
Cast off.

TO FINISH

With centre of cast off edge of sleeve to shoulder markers, sew on sleeves. Join side and sleeve seams.

RIBBON EDGING

Measure around the cuffs and the front/back neck edge, then cut the ribbon into three lengths allowing an extra 6cm for each cuff and 20cm for the neck. Run a line of long tacking stitches along one edge of each ribbon length, pull up slightly to gather and stitch to the inside of the cuffs, front and neck edges, distributing the soft gathers evenly.

hooded kaftan

MEASUREMENTS

To fit ages	3–6	6–12	12–18	18–24	months

ACTUAL MEASUREMENTS

Chest	52	55	61	64	cm
Length to shoulder	26	30	34	37	cm
Sleeve length	15	17	19	22	cm

MATERIALS

- 4(5:6:7) 50g balls of Debbie Bliss cotton cashmere double knitting in Stone
- Pair each of 3¼mm and 3¾mm knitting needles
- Small amounts of embroidery threads
- Embroidery needle

TENSION

22 sts and 30 rows to 10cm square over st st using 3¾mm needles.

ABBREVIATIONS

See page 121.

BACK

With 3¼mm needles, cast on 59(63:69:73) sts.
K 3 rows.
Change to 3¾mm needles.
1st row (right side) K to end.
2nd row K2, p to last 2 sts, k2.
Rep the last 2 rows twice more.
Beg with a k row, work in st st until back measures 15(18:20:22)cm from cast on edge, ending with a p row.
Shape armholes
Cast off 3(3:4:4) sts at beg of next 2 rows.
Dec one st at each end of the next and 1(2:2:3) foll alt rows. 49(51:55:57) sts. **
Cont straight until back measures 26(30:34:37)cm from cast on edge, ending with a p row.
Shape shoulders
Cast off 10(11:12:13) sts at beg of next 2 rows.
Cast off rem 29(29:31:31) sts.

FRONT

Work as given for Back to **.
Cont straight until front measures 18(21:24:27)cm from cast on edge, ending with a p row.
Front opening
Next row K23(24:26:27), turn and work on these sts only for first side of front, leave rem sts on a spare needle.
Work straight until front measures same as Back to shoulder, ending at side edge.
Shape shoulder
Cast off 10(11:12:13) sts at beg of next row.
P 1 row.
Leave rem 13(13:14:14) sts on a spare needle.
With right side facing, rejoin yarn to rem sts, cast off 3 sts, k to end.
Work straight until front measures same as Back to shoulder, ending at side edge.
Shape shoulder
Cast off 10(11:12:13) sts at beg of next row.
Do not cut yarn, leave sts on needle.

hooded kaftan

KEY

 FRENCH KNOT IN ROSE

STRAIGHT STITCH IN FUCHSIA

STRAIGHT STITCH IN ROSE

CHAIN STITCH IN MALLARD

CHAIN STITCH IN PALE BLUE

FRENCH KNOT IN WHITE

HOOD

Join shoulder seams.
With right side facing and 3¾mm needles, k across 13(13:14:14) sts from right front spare needle, cast on 41(41:44:44) sts, k across 13(13:14:14) sts from left front needle. 67(67:72:72) sts.
Cont in st st and work 3 rows.
Inc row K4, m1, k to last 4 sts, m1, k4.
Work 5 rows straight.
Rep the last 6 rows 9(10:11:12) times more.
Cast off.

SLEEVES

With 3¼mm needles, cast on 35(37:43:45) sts.
K 3 rows.
Change to 3¾mm needles.
Beg with a k row, work in st st, inc one st at each end of the 3rd and every foll 4th row until there are 53(59:69:75) sts.
Cont straight until sleeve measures 15(17:19:22)cm from cast on edge, ending with a wrong side row.
Shape top
Cast off 3(3:4:4) sts at beg of next 2 rows.
Dec one st at each end of the next and 1(2:2:3) foll alt rows. 43(47:55:59) sts.
Cast off.

FRONT EDGINGS

With right side facing and 3¼mm needles, pick up and k70(78:86:92) sts along each front edge.
K 3 rows.
Cast off.

EMBROIDERY

Following the diagrams on page 101, work embroidery around the neck and sleeve edges.

TO FINISH

Sew sleeves into armholes. Join sleeve seams. Join side seams to top of opening. Join hood seam. Sew row ends of front edging to sts cast off at centre front. Sew cast on edge of hood to cast off sts at back neck.

hooded kaftan

carrying bag

MEASUREMENTS
Approximately 40.5 x 76cm

MATERIALS
- Eight 50g balls Debbie Bliss cashmerino aran in Cream
- Pair of 5mm knitting needles
- 80cm of 90-cm wide fabric
- 1m of ribbon
- Sewing thread and needle

TENSION
18 sts and 32 rows to 10cm square over moss stitch using 5mm needles.

ABBREVIATIONS
See page 121.

TO MAKE
With 5mm needles, cast on 137 sts.
Moss st row K1, [p1, k1] to end.
Work in moss st until bag measures 81cm from cast on edge.
Cast off.

TO FINISH
Lay the knitted piece on top of the fabric, then adding 2cm all around, cut the fabric to size. With right sides together, fold the fabric in half. Matching the two shorter ends and taking a 2cm seam, stitch from the fold to the edges, across the bottom of the doubled fabric to form the base of the bag and continue the seam for 22cm up the side. Press the seam open and continue to press the edges under around the remaining fabric, folding the top corners to neaten. Cut the ribbon into four pieces and stitch in pairs to each side of the bag. Fold the knitted piece in half matching the cast on and cast off edges. Stitch the lower edge and continue the seam for 22cm along the side. Insert the knitted lining in the bag and slip stitch all around the open edges.

argyle cardigan

To fit ages	0–3	3–6	6–9	9–12	12–24	months

ACTUAL MEASUREMENTS

Chest	48	53	58	63	68	cm
Length to shoulder	22	25	27	29	33	cm
Sleeve length	13	15	17	19	22	cm

MATERIALS

- 2(3:3:3:4) 50g balls of Debbie Bliss baby cashmerino in Wedgwood (A)
- Small amounts in each of White (B) and Indigo (C)
- Pair each of 3mm and 3¼mm knitting needles
- 3¼mm circular knitting needle
- 6(6:6:7:7) buttons

TENSION

25 sts and 34 rows to 10cm square over st st using 3¼mm needles.

ABBREVIATIONS

See page 121.

CHART NOTE

When working from chart read right side (k) rows from right to left and wrong side (p) rows from left to right. Work between lines for correct size, repeating the 26 st pattern repeat. When working colour motifs, use separate small balls of each contrast yarn for each area of colour and twist yarns on wrong side when changing colour to avoid holes.

BACK AND FRONTS

With 3¼mm circular needle and A, cast on 116(128:144:152:168) sts.
Work backwards and forwards in rows as follows:
1st row (right side) K3, * p2, k2; rep from * to last 5 sts, p2, k3.
2nd row P3, * k2, p2; rep from * to last 5 sts, k2, p3.
Rep these 2 rows twice more, increasing 3(4:1:6:3) sts evenly across last row. 119(132:145:158:171) sts.
Beg with a k row work 4 rows in st st.
Cont in st st and work 11 rows from chart.
Cont in A only until back measures 13(15:16:17:19)cm from cast on edge, ending with a p row.
Divide for back and fronts
Next row K26(30:32:35:38), leave these sts on a holder for right front, cast off next 6(6:8:8:10) sts, k until there are 55(60:65:72:75) sts on needle, leave these sts on a holder for back, cast off next 6(6:8:8:10) sts, k to end.
Cont on last set of 26(30:32:35:38) sts only for left front.
Dec one st at armhole edge on 3(4:4:5:5) foll alt rows. 23(26:28:30:33) sts.
Cont straight until work measures 18(20:22:23:27)cm from cast on edge, ending with a p row.
Shape neck
Next row K to last 4(5:5:5:6) sts, turn and leave these sts on a holder.
Dec one st at neck edge on every row until 13(14:15:16:17) sts rem.
Cont straight until work measures 22(25:27:29:33)cm from cast on edge, ending at armhole edge.

a r g y l e   c a r d i g a n

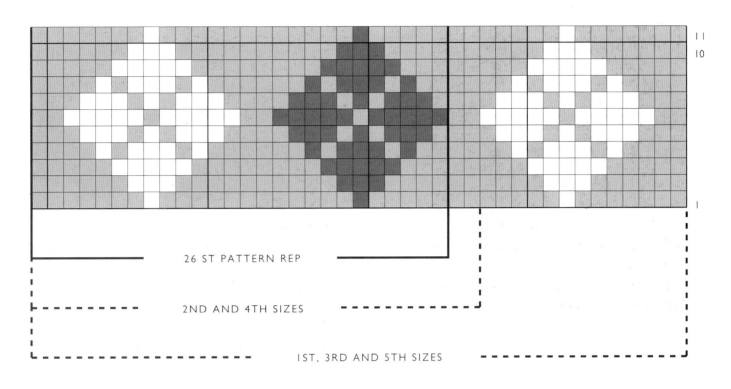

11
10
1

26 ST PATTERN REP

2ND AND 4TH SIZES

1ST, 3RD AND 5TH SIZES

KEY

A

B

C

Shape shoulder

Cast off.

With wrong side facing, rejoin yarn to centre 55(60:65:72:75) sts for back, p to end.

Shape armholes

Dec one st at each end of next row and 2(3:3:4:4) foll alt rows. 49(52:57:62:65) sts.

Cont straight until back measures same as Left Front to shoulder, ending with a wrong side row.

Shape shoulders

Cast off 13(14:15:16:17) sts at beg of next 2 rows.

Leave rem 23(24:27:30:31) sts on a holder.

With wrong side facing, work across last set of 26(30:32:35:38) sts for right front.

Dec one st at armhole edge on next row and 2(3:3:4:4) foll alt rows. 23(26:28:30:33) sts.

Cont straight until work measures 18(20:22:23:27)cm from cast on edge, ending with a p row.

Shape neck

Next row K4(5:5:5:6) sts, leave these sts on a holder, k to end.

Dec one st at neck edge on every row until 13(14:15:16:17) sts rem.

Cont straight until work measures 22(25:27:29:33)cm from cast on edge, ending at armhole edge.

Shape shoulder

Cast off.

With 3mm needles and A, cast on 34(34:38:38:42) sts.

1st row (right side) K2, * p2, k2; rep from * to end.

2nd row P2, * k2, p2; rep from * to end.

Change to 3¼mm needles.

Rep these last 2 rows once more and inc 2 sts evenly across last row. 36(36:40:40:44) sts.

Beg with a k row, work in st st and inc one st at each end of the 3rd and every foll 4th row until there are 52(56:62:68:76) sts.

Cont straight until sleeve measures 13(15:17:19:22)cm from cast on edge, ending with a p row.

Cast off 4(4:5:5:6) sts at beg of next 2 rows.

Dec one st at each end of the next row and 2(3:3:4:4) foll alt rows. 38(40:44:48:54) sts.

Cast off.

argyle cardigan

NECKBAND

Join shoulder seams.

With right side facing, 3mm needles and A, slip 4(5:5:5:6) sts from right front holder onto a needle, pick up and k16(16:17:17:18) sts up right front neck to shoulder, k across 23(24:27:30:31) sts of back neck and inc 1(2:1:2:1) sts evenly, pick up and k16(16:17:17:18) sts down left front neck, then k4(5:5:5:6) sts from left front neck holder. 64(68:72:76:80) sts.

Beg with a 2nd row, work 5 rows in rib as given for Back and Fronts.

Cast off in rib.

BUTTON BAND

With right side facing, 3mm needles and A, pick up and k54(58:66:70:78) sts along left front edge.

Beg with a 2nd row, work 5 rows in rib as given for Sleeves.

Cast off in rib.

BUTTONHOLE BAND

With right side facing, 3mm needles and A, pick up and k54(58:66:70:78) sts along right front edge.

Beg with a 2nd row, work one row in rib as given for Sleeves.

Buttonhole row (right side) Rib 3(3:4:4:2), [rib 2 tog, yf, rib 7(8:9:8:10) sts] 5(5:5:6:6) times, rib 2 tog, yf, rib 4(3:5:4:2).

Rib 2 rows.

Cast off in rib.

TO FINISH

Join sleeve seams. Sew sleeves into armholes.

Sew on buttons.

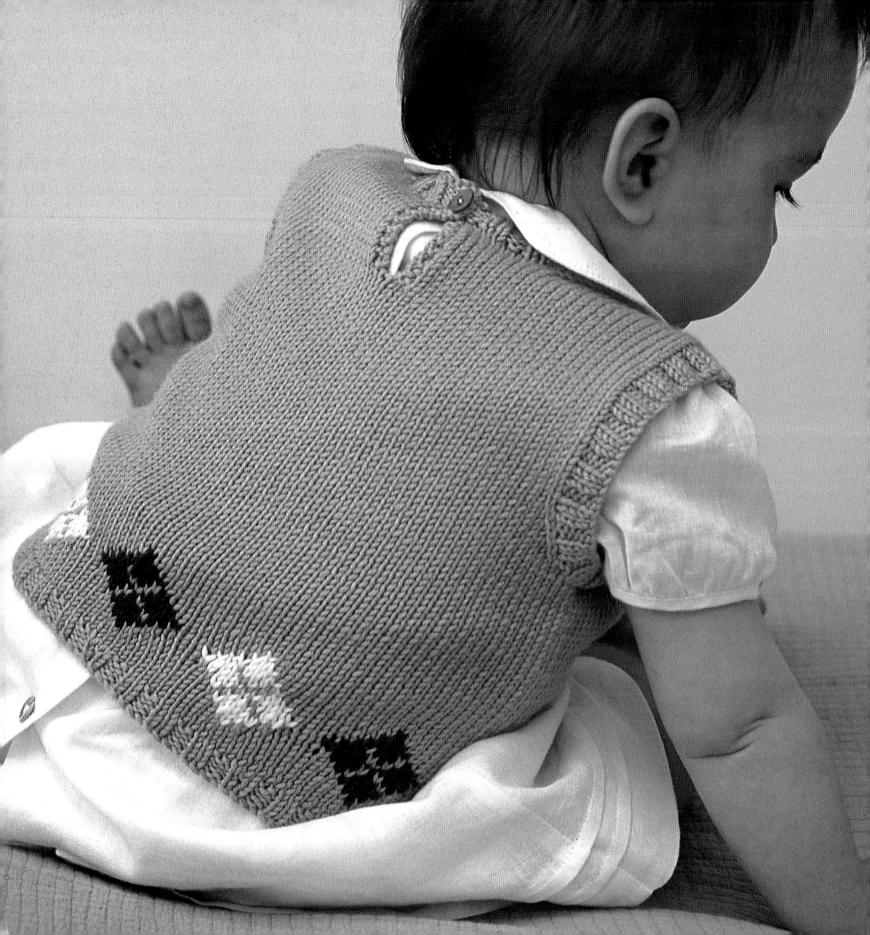

argyle slipover

MEASUREMENTS

To fit ages		0–3	3–6	6–9	9–12	12–24	months

ACTUAL MEASUREMENTS

Chest		45	50	53	58	63	cm
Length to shoulder		21	24	26	28	32	cm

MATERIALS

- 2(2:3:3:3) 50g balls of Debbie Bliss baby cashmerino in Wedgwood (A)
- Small amounts in each of White (B) and Indigo (C)
- Pair each of 3mm and 3¼mm knitting needles
- 3mm circular knitting needle
- One small button

TENSION

25 sts and 34 rows to 10cm square over st st using 3¼mm needles.

ABBREVIATIONS

See page 121.

CHART NOTE

Use separate small balls of contrast yarn for each motif and twist yarns at colour change to avoid holes. Work between lines for correct size, repeating the 26 st pattern repeat.

BACK

With 3mm needles and A, cast on 58(62:66:74:78) sts.
1st row K2, * p2, k2; rep from * to end.
2nd row P2, * k2, p2; rep from * to end.
Rep the last 2 rows once more, and inc 1(3:3:1:3) sts evenly across last row. 59(65:69:75:81) sts.
Change to 3¼mm needles.
Beg with a k row, work 4 rows in st st.
Work 11 rows in st st from chart.
Cont in st st and A and work until back measures 11(13:14:15:18)cm from cast on edge, ending with a p row.
Shape armholes
Cast off 3(4:4:5:5) sts at beg of next 2 rows.
Dec one st at each end of the next and 3(3:4:4:5) foll alt rows. 45(49:51:55:59) sts. **
Cont in st st until back measures 15(17:19:22:26)cm from cast on edge, ending with a p row.
Back neck opening
1st row K23(25:26:28:30) sts, turn and work on these

sts for first side of neck shaping, leave rem sts on a spare needle.
2nd row K2, p to end.
3rd row K to end.
Rep the last 2 rows until back measures 19(22:24:26:30)cm from cast on edge, ending with a wrong side row.
Shape neck
Next row K15(16:17:18:19) sts, turn, leave rem 8(9:9:10:11) sts on a safety pin.
Dec 1 st at neck edge on next 4 rows.
11(12:13:14:15) sts.
Work 3 rows in st st.
Cast off for shoulder.
With right side facing, rejoin yarn to sts on spare needle, cast on one st, k to end.
2nd row P to last 2 sts, k2.
3rd row K to end.
Rep the last 2 rows until back measures 19(22:24:26:30)cm from cast on edge, ending with a k row.
Shape neck
Next row P15(16:17:18:19) sts, turn, leave rem 8(9:9:10:11) sts on a safety pin.
Dec 1 st at neck edge on next 4 rows.
11(12:13:14:15) sts.
Work 2 rows in st st.
Cast off for shoulder.

argyle slipover

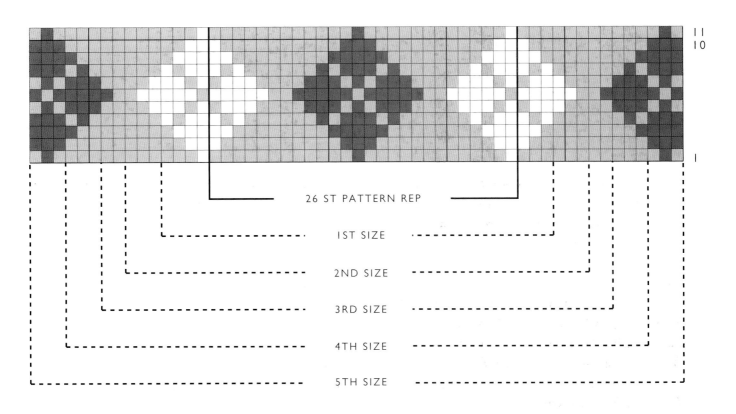

11
10

1

26 ST PATTERN REP

1ST SIZE

2ND SIZE

3RD SIZE

4TH SIZE

5TH SIZE

KEY

A

B

C

FRONT

Work as given for Back to **.

Cont in st st until front measures 15(18:20:21:25)cm from cast on edge, ending with a p row.

Shape neck

Next row K17(18:19:20:21) sts, turn and work on these sts for first side of front neck, leave rem sts on a spare needle.

Dec 1 st at neck edge on next and every foll alt row until 11(12:13:14:15) sts rem.

Work straight until front measures same as Back to shoulder, ending with a p row.

Cast off.

With right side facing, slip centre 11(13:13:15:17) sts onto a holder, rejoin yarn to rem sts on spare needle, k to end.

Complete to match first side of neck, reversing shaping.

NECKBAND

Join shoulder seams.

With right side facing, 3mm circular needle and A, slip 8(9:9:10:11) sts from left back onto needle. pick up and k8 sts up left back neck, 15(15:15:17:17) sts down left side of front neck, k across 11(13:13:15:17) sts from front neck holder, pick up and k15(15:15:17:17) sts up right side of front neck, 9 sts down right back neck, k across 8(9:9:10:11) sts from back neck holder. 74(78:78:86:90) sts.

1st row P2, * k2, p2; rep from * to end.

2nd row K2, * p2, k2; rep from * to end.

Rep the last 2 rows once more.

Cast off in rib

ARMBANDS

With right side facing, 3mm needles and A, pick up and k62(70:74:78:86) sts.

Work 4 rows in rib as given for Back.

Cast off in rib.

TO FINISH

Join side and armband seams. Make a button loop on left back neckband. Sew on button.

argyle slipover

picture index

8 Eyelet vest.

To fit ages 6–12, 12–18, 18–24, 24–36 months

12 Garter-stitch blanket.

14 Ribbed jacket.

To fit ages 0–3, 3–6, 6–9, 9–12, 12–24 months

18 Hooded sweater.

To fit ages 0–3, 3–6, 6–9, 9–12, 12–24 months

22 Embroidered kimono. To fit ages 3–6, 6–12, 12–18 months

28 Ribbon-edged cardigan. To fit ages 0–3, 3–6, 6–9, 9–12, 12–24 months

32 Rabbit.

36 Alphabet sweater.

To fit ages 3, 6, 12, 24 months

42 Check and cross-stitch jacket. To fit ages 6, 18, 24 months

48 Ribbon-tied dress.

To fit ages 3–6, 6–12, 12–18, 18–24 months

 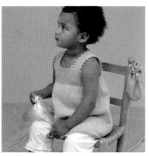  

52 Shawl.

56 Picot dress and bag. To fit ages 3–6, 9–12, 12–18, 18–24 months

62 Velvet-edged jacket. To fit ages 0–3, 3–6, 6–9, 9–12, 12–24 months

68 Fair isle top. To fit ages 6–12, 12–18, 18–24 months

74 Bow-tied bolero. To fit ages 6–9, 9–12, 12–18, 18–24, 24–36 months

78 Beaded cardigan. To fit ages 12–18, 18–24, 24–36 months

86 Sampler blanket.

92 Organza-edged cardigan. To fit ages 3–6, 6–9, 9–12, 12–24 months

98 Hooded kaftan. To fit ages 3–6, 6–12, 12–18, 18–24 months

104 Carrying bag.

106 Argyle cardigan. To fit ages 0–3, 3–6, 6–9, 9–12, 12–24 months

112 Argyle slipover. To fit ages 0–3, 3–6, 6–9, 9–12, 12–24 months

basic information

KNITTING ABBREVIATIONS

alt	alternate		pfb	purl into front and back of next st
beg	beginning		psso	pass slipped st over
cont	continue		rem	remaining
dec	decrease		rep	repeat
foll	following		skpo	slip 1, knit 1, pass slipped stitch over
inc	increase		sl	slip
k	knit		st(s)	stitch(es)
kfb	knit into front and back of next st		st st	stocking stitch
m1	make one by picking up the loop lying between st just worked and next st and working into back of it		tbl	through back loop
			tog	together
patt	pattern		yf	yarn forward
p	purl		yon	yarn over needle
			yrn	yarn round needle

READING PATTERN INSTRUCTIONS

Figures for larger sizes are given in round ( ) brackets. Where only one figure appears this means that it applies to all the sizes. Work the figures given in square [ ] brackets the number of times quoted afterwards. Where 0 appears no stitches or rows are worked for this size.

The quantities of yarn stated in the pattern are based on the yarn amounts used by the knitter of the original garment. Yarn amounts therefore should be considered approximate as a slight variation in tension can make the difference between using fewer or more balls or hanks than that stated. My patterns quote the actual chest measurements of the garment and not the child, check these measurements first as you may wish to make a smaller or larger garment for the age of the child.

TENSION

Tension is one of the most important aspects of hand knitting. Tension is the number of stitches and rows per centimetre that should be obtained using the same yarn, needles and stitch as the pattern requires and will always be quoted at the beginning of a knitting pattern. A variation of stitches and rows over a certain measurement can make the difference between a smaller or larger garment than the size that you are knitting, a tighter fabric that is stiff and uncomfortable to wear or a looser one that is unstable and stretches. A garment has been designed with the proportions very much in mind; if you have a different stitch tension giving a wider or narrower width, but the length of the design is worked in measurement rather than rows, you will have a different shaped garment than the original design.

Always make a tension square before you start the garment. Knit a sample approximately 13 cm square using the needles and yarns quoted in the tension note at the beginning of the pattern. Smooth out the finished square on a flat surface and leave it to relax for a while. To check the stitch tension, place a tape measure or ruler horizontally on the sample and mark out 10 cm with pins. Count the number of stitches within the pins. To check the row tension, place the tape measure vertically and mark out 10 cm with pins. Count the rows within the pins. If the number of stitches and rows is greater than that quoted it means your tension is tighter and you need to use larger needles to create bigger stitches. If there are fewer stitches and rows, try a smaller needle to make smaller stitches. If you are only able to obtain either the correct stitch or row tension, it is the stitch tension that is the most important to get right, as often patterns are calculated in measurements rather than rows.

CARE OF GARMENTS

Always check the label for washing instructions. All the yarns used in this book are machine-washable, but with small garments like these it does not take much effort to handwash them, which I always prefer. Before washing make a note of the measurement, and

basic information

after washing dry the garment flat on a towel, patting it back into the shape if excess moisture is making it stretch slightly. Take care not to wring or rub the fabric and do not be tempted to dry it quickly with direct heat, such as a radiator.

YARN

Do check dye lot numbers when you are buying your yarn. Yarns are dyed in batches, and the colour can vary between one lot and another. Buy an extra ball if you sometimes use more balls then the amount quoted in the pattern; you may find that if you go back to your retailer later to buy extra, it is no longer the same dye lot and there will be a variation in the shade, which although you can't see it in the ball, really shows up when knitted.

When buying yarn always try to buy the yarn that I have used in the pattern, as I will have designed the garment specifically with that yarn in mind. It may be because a particular yarn, such as a cotton, shows a subtle stitch, such as moss stitch, beautifully, and this will be lost if an inferior yarn is substituted. A hooded top in a cashmere mix is soft and snugly, but in a harder yarn it could be rough against a baby's skin.

If, however, you do decide to use a substitute yarn, always make sure that you can obtain the same tension and where possible choose the same fibre content. Check the metreage on the ball band and if there are fewer metres in the ball than in the original yarn, you may need to buy extra balls.

The following information is a description of my yarns that have been used in this book and a guide to their weight and metreage.

■ DEBBIE BLISS CASHMERINO ARAN.
A 55% merino wool, 33% microfibre and 12% cashmere mix. Approx. 90m/50g ball.

■ DEBBIE BLISS BABY CASHMERINO.
The same luxury mix as above, but a lightweight yarn, between a 4ply and a double knitting. Approx. 125m/50g ball.

■ DEBBIE BLISS COTTON CASHMERE.
85% cotton, 15% cashmere, in a double knitting weight. Approx. 95m/50g ball.

SUPPLIERS

For suppliers of Debbie Bliss yarns please contact:

USA
Knitting Fever Inc.
P.O. Box 502
Roosevelt, New York 11575
Tel: (516) 546 3600
Fax: (516) 546 6871
www.knittingfever.com

Canada
Diamond Yarns Ltd, 155 Martin Ross Avenue, Unit 3, Toronto, Ontario M3J 2L9
Tel: 001 416 736 6111
www.diamondyarn.com

Mexico
Red Color, S.A. DE CV. San Antonio 105, Col. Santa Maria, Monterrey, N.L. 64650
Tel: +52 818 173 3700
e-mail: Abremer@starsoft.co.mx

Japan
Eisaku Noro & Co Ltd., 55 Shimoda Ohibino Azaichou, Ichinomita Aichi, 4910105.
Tel: +81 52 203 5100
www.eisakunoro.com

UK
Designer Yarns Ltd, Units 8-10 Newbridge Industrial Estate, Pitt Street, Keighley, W. Yorkshire, BD21 4PQ
Tel: +44 (0)1535 664222
Fax: +44 (01535) 664333
www.designeryarns.uk.com
e-mail: jane@designeryarns.uk.com

Germany/Austria/Switzerland
Designer Yarns, Handelsagentur Klaus Koch, Mauritius Str. 130 50226 Frechen.
Tel: +49 2234 205453
Fax: +49 2234 205456
www.designeryarns.de

France
Elle Tricote, 8 Rue du Coq, (Petit France) 67000 Strasbourg.
Tel: +33 (0)388 230313
www.elletricote.com.fr

Spain
Oyambre, Pau Claris 145, 08009 Barcelona
Tel: +34 934 872672
e-mail: oyambre@oyambreonline.com

Belgium/Holland
Pavan, Meerlaanstraat 73, Oostrezele 9860
Tel: +32 9221 8594
Fax +32 9221 5662
e-mail: pavan@pandora.be

Sweden
Hamilton Design, Långgatan 20, SE-64730, Mariefred.
Tel/fax: +46 (0)159 12006
www.hamiltondesign.biz

Australia
Sunspun, 185 Canterbury Road, Canterbury VIC 3126
Tel: +61 (0)3 9830 1609
e-mail: shop@sunspun.com.au

Jo Sharp Pty Ltd., P.O. Box 1018, Fremantle, WA 6959
Tel: +61 08 9430 9699
e-mail: yarn@josharp.com.au

Denmark
Strikkeboden, Krystalgade 16, 1172 Copenhagen K
Tel: +45 4583 0127
e-mail: jens.toersleff@get2net.dk

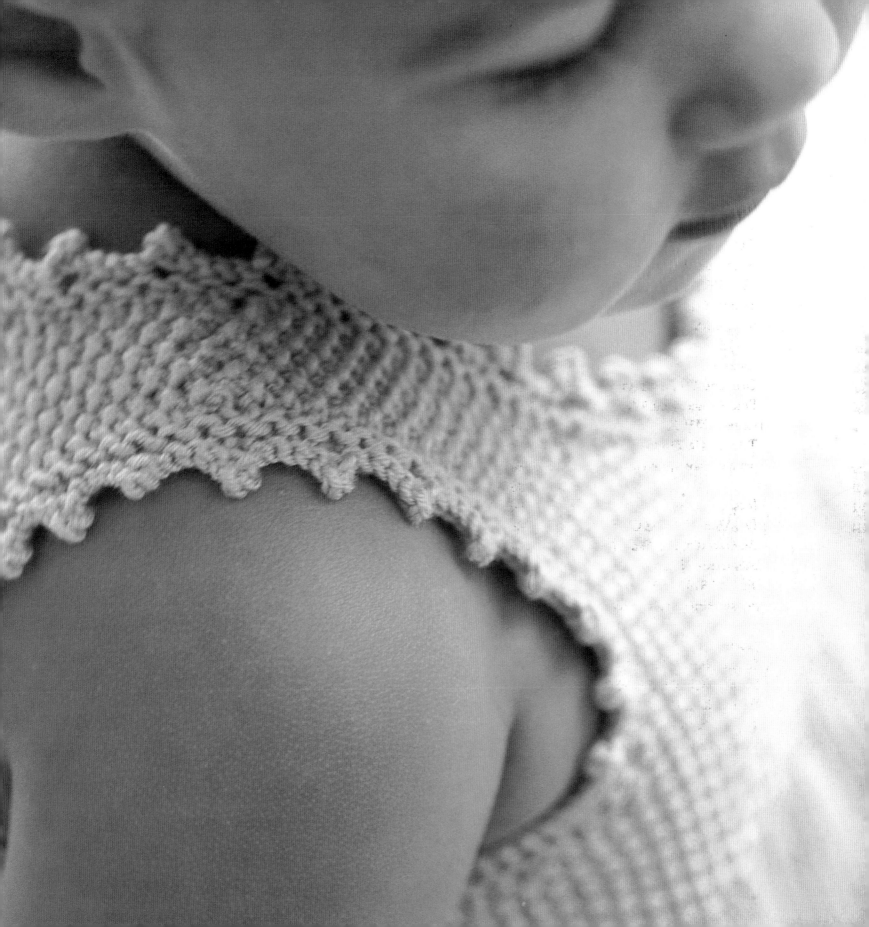

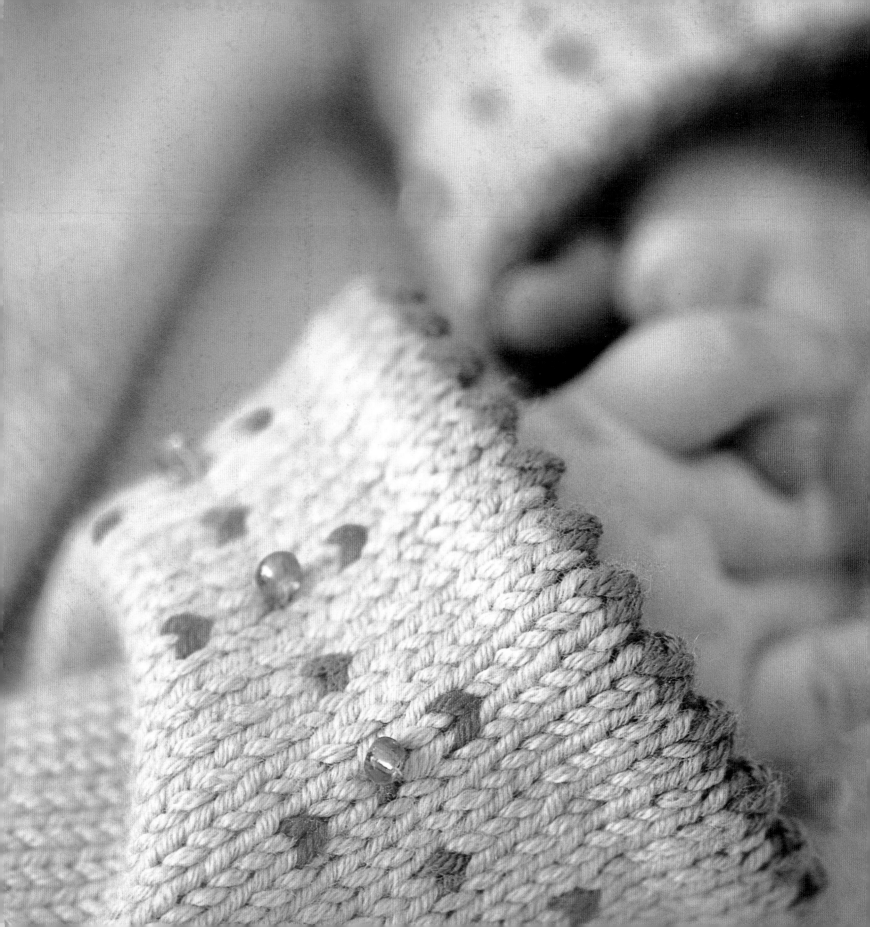

ACKNOWLEDGEMENTS

This book would not have been possible without the invaluable collaboration of the following:

Rosy Tucker, for pattern checking and creative contribution.

Penny Hill for pattern compiling and checking.

Melody Griffiths for her design involvement.

Sandra Lousada for her beautiful photography and her assistants, Anne, Bridget and Nicola.

Sammie Bell for the lovely styling.

Kate Haxell for being a great editor and Elvis for being a great dog.

Marie Clayton and Colin Ziegler for making it happen.

Roger Hammond@Blue Gum for the great book design.

Luise Roberts for the charts and artwork.

The brilliant knitters who work to impossible deadlines; Brenda Bostock, Cynthia Brent, Jill Borley, Sally Buss, Pat Church, Jacqui Dunt, Penny Hill, Shirley Kennet, Janet Kopinski, Maisie Lawrence, Gwen Radford, Jean Trehane and Frances Wallace.

The models, Ella, Afia, Poppy, Oliver, Charlotte, Isabelle, Sam, Amira, Wilf, Iris and Simah.

My wonderful agent, Heather Jeeves.

The knitters, retailers and distributors who support my yarns and books.

The day bed used in some of the photographs is from www.bumpstuff.com

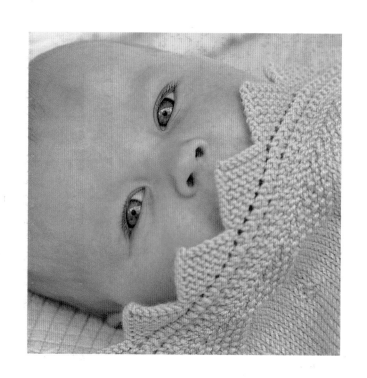